The Great Physician

by Charles S. Price
(First published in 1924)

**For more great Christian classics that have been
out-of-print for far too long, visit us online at:**

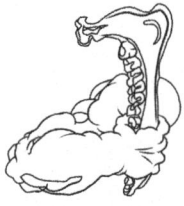

JawboneDigital.com

To every seeker after truth,
to every hungry heart in need of
the bread of life,
to every suffering body in need of
THE GREAT PHYSICIAN
this book is prayerfully and lovingly dedicated.

ISBN: 1548342904
ISBN-13: 978-1548342906

Copyright © 2017 Jawbone Digital
Yuma, Colorado
All rights reserved.

TABLE OF CONTENTS

Chapter 1
The Great Physician
1

Chapter 2
The Scriptures on Divine Healing
9

Chapter 3
How to Receive Your Healing
34

Chapter 4
How to Keep Your Healing
60

Chapter 5
The Jericho Road
77

Chapter 6
A Model Revival
94

CHAPTER 1
THE GREAT PHYSICIAN

Night! Night! Night! How deep its shades, how dark its ways; how hidden its paths, and how clothed in mystery its purposes; yet it is out of that night that there steals the roseate dews of early morn and it is out of its depths that there comes the signal glimmer of twilight that calls for the birdsong and the break of day. Has the path been dark, my brother, and in its depths have your weary feet oft stumbled and erred? Has the road been weary and the long night dreary, and in the perplexity of your heart have you cried that eternal "WHY"? Then, my brother, lift up your head again, and look eastward toward the land of the resurrection hopes, and before long you will see the dawning of a happy day; for the Sun of Righteousness will arise with healing in His wings. Bethlehem's Star of Hope will change to the glory of noonday for the Light of the World Himself is knocking with nail-pierced hand at the portals of your heart. Wherever the Prince of Glory goes the dark shadows flee; wherever He lays His loving hand wounded hearts throb with the impulse of new life; wherever His voice is heard, in the palace of the rich or the hovel of the poor, He brings comfort and sunshine and gladness and the dayspring from on high bursts in love and glory over these poor hearts of ours. There is hope for you... in Jesus. There is life for you... in Jesus. There is healing for you... in Jesus. There is all that you need for body, soul and spirit... in Jesus.

We are coming to you to point out the one way out. To show you the only solution to your difficulties; to tell you that at the foot of an old rugged Cross you can lay life's burdens down and still find in Jesus the rest to your weary souls. I am praying for the leadership of the Holy Spirit as I write that as I take you over the steps toward the desire of your heart you may see—always—only JESUS.

The first thing we need, and indeed the one great essential in every life is a real born-again experience. Not an empty shallow profession of a knowledge of scripture, but the possession of a real living Christ who dwells in your heart by faith and who walks and communes with you along life's pathway and tells you that you are His, and He is yours forever and forever. Many professed Christians know ABOUT Christ who do not really know Him; many have a form of Godliness but deny the power of a life that is hid with Christ in God. Real salvation is only experienced and can never be explained. No subscription to any code of ethics, no intellectual assent to any dogma, no mental appreciation of any truth can in itself bring about the salvation of the soul. Only the simple faith of a man who stakes his all on the veracity of the Word and who stands upon the integrity of the promises, can ever bring about the wondrous change in the heart that the Bible calls salvation. No amount of reasoning will ever suffice. Spiritual things are spiritually discerned. No man can see the truth in the word or behold the glory of a personal saving Christ who has not a spiritual vision. No man can hear the voice of Jesus, sweet as bells at evening pealing who has not a spiritual ear. No man can understand the power of redeeming grace who has not had the renewed mind and experienced within the confines of his own life the transforming power of God.

It took the dynamic of saving grace to change Saul of Tarsus into the indomitable hero of the cross defending his faith before Agrippa. It took the magnetism of a love that was divine to draw Peter from the fishing nets of Galilee to the ways that the Master went. It took a salvation that was real to transform a Magdalene or to change a heart of stone. Not content with worshipping from afar at the feet of a historic Christ we must KNOW Him whom to know is life eternal. Oh, to forget the world and its cares; to cast aside if needs be even reason and our pre-conceived ideas of God and things become as the Savior Himself once said "as a little child." Then to throw ourselves in the childlike faith on to the sea of His infinite love and BELIEVE, BELIEVE, BELIEVE. In these days of morbid materialism and so-called rationalism that destroys all vital faith, the mind and heart of man has been demanding proof. "The wind bloweth where it listeth and thou hearest the sound thereof but canst not tell whence it cometh or whither it goeth, so is ever one that is born of the Spirit."

Proof! We demand it and, praise the Lord, we can have it! The proof of the pudding is in the eating. The proof of salvation is in its experience. Without the experience it can never be proved and we shall search in vain for our truth until we come unto Him who said, "I am the way, the TRUTH and the life." What a glorious proof it is when at last He comes. Bound by the fetters of habit and of sin, in our extremity we seek the Lord. We grasp at His golden promise, and hardly believe that it can really mean us. We have tried the broken cisterns and have found that their waters failed. We have found in the world in which we live not a ray of sunshine, not a sunbeam of hope. "This poor man cried and the Lord heard him and DELIVERED him out of all his trouble." What a deliverance. The Lion of the tribe of Judah breaks every chain. Habits are broken and sin fetters are snapped. Through the portals of the heart walks the Son of God. The dungeon flames with light. Old things are passing away and behold all things are becoming new. The heart changes from stone to flesh. The glory of the Lord bursts upon the soul until His praises leave our lips and the glory of the Lord is revealed in the land of the living. One experience may not parallel another. One conversion may not be like another, but one thing is sure; there is taught in God's word a clearcut, definite, concrete experience of sins forgiven and a change of heart and no man should be content or rest smugly satisfied with his own condition until the knowledge of that change is a real experience in his life. He comes to convert, to change, to transform and so wonderfully does the center of the life change that some men have said they first began to live when He came to abide and to love.

What a price He paid for our salvation and joy. "Without the shedding of blood there is no remission of sins"; without the cross there could never be a crown; with the agony of His death we could never know the glory of our Eternal life. So it is that you who seek a healing Christ must first find Him as a Savior; you who would have Him bind up the wounds of a body that is weary and tired and worn must first have Him bind up the wounds of your heart and proclaim Him the King of your life, your Savior, your Friend and your Lord. Can we ask Him to heal a body that will not be dedicated in service unto Him? Dare we ask Him for healing virtue when our hearts want none of His saving grace? No! It cannot be. When we come it must be with the prayer, "Dear Lord, I am Thine. All that I am, all that I ever hope to be, is Thine for time and eternity. Believing Thy word, dear Lord, I come to claim my healing."

"Just as I am without one plea
But that They blood was shed for me
And that Thou bidst me come to Thee
Oh, Lamb of God, I come."

CHAPTER 2
THE SCRIPTURES ON DIVINE HEALING

The first questions that must naturally come to the mind when thinking about the healing of the body must be, "What scriptural authority is there for people praying for the sick in these days," and "What does the Bible teach about divine healing methods?" One thing is sure: if we have no scriptural authority we should never pray for the sick. If there is no clear Bible teaching on the question of our healing we should never claim it. The Word of God is a lamp unto our feet and a light unto our path. When we go outside the word for our experiences we inevitably meet with disaster and make ultimate shipwreck of our faith. But if it is in the word why not claim it and appropriate it unto ourselves. Why claim part of the promises and let the rest go by? Why be satisfied with a part salvation when the Bible teaches us there is a salvation wonderful, real and complete? As a matter of fact, the very center of this whole movement that is sweeping the continent and has leaped across the waters and is traveling with the rapidity of a prairie fire in lands across the sea is that the WORD OF GOD IS TRUE. The battle cry that has been raised it "Back to the old standards; back to the faith of our fathers. Remove not the old landmarks and take not away the promises of God. His promises are sure and His word is Truth." How sweet are those promises. How steadfast and sure they have remained all during the years that have sped by, ever giving to the needy sons of Adam's race, hope in the midst of despair and a way out of every difficulty. Heaven and earth may pass away but those promises remain forever, and happy is the man who has discovered that the days of his life can be spent "Standing on the promises of God."

"In the beginning God created." With these words does the old Book introduce God. He was the Creator, the maker of the heavens and the earth and without Him was not anything made that is made. His creation was good, pure and a reflection of Himself. It was His handiwork and all the created spoke of the glory of the Creator. In the first Edenic home God placed man and gave him dominion over all the beasts of the field and the birds of the air. Created in the image of God he was the companion of the divine and walked and talked with God in the cool of the evening time. Happiness was God's gift and the presence of God was man's pleasure and privilege. No sickness or death or pain came into his life to mar and to spoil it but, man, created a little lower than the angels, lived in the sunshine of God's presence and the created and the Creator shared alike in the Edenic glory and splendor. Say not that God created pain. Say not that God was or is the author of sickness or that death came stalking into the garden by the command of the Lord. Say rather that man, possessed of the power of choice, a free moral agent, with authority to reject or to accept, chose the ways of disobedience and transgressed the laws of God. With diabolic cunning the devil came into the garden and persuaded Eve that the word of God was not true. That was the blackest lie the devil ever told and he has never invented a blacker one from that day to this. No matter where that story is told; in the heart of the infidel, or in the pulpit of a church, the devil is always satisfied. If he can get you to believe that the word is not true his work is done and done well. Whenever and wherever the devil can get you to doubt the word of God the result is always the same: an ultimate shipwreck of your faith and heart oppressed by doubts and fears.

Eve, poor foolish Eve, doubted God's word and sinned. For sin is disobedience and disobedience always carries its penalty. The mandate of God had gone forth "The soul that sinneth it shall die." So it was that death came into the world and so it was that sickness came into the garden with sin to blight and to mar and spoil the wonderful creation of God. Do not say it was God's purpose and do not believe it was God's plan, but rather say that of his own free will and volition man chose the ways of death by willfully disobeying God. Then and there God commenced that great plan of redemption. Man was to be won back, Eden was to be restored, sins were to be forgiven and sicknesses were to be healed, and so it was that God commenced to lead His people along certain steps of progression and understanding until the Lamb slain from the foundation of the world was to be made that atoning sacrifice on Calvary. It is very clear to the student of scripture that even in Old Testament times God the Father, who, in later years sent His Son into the world to DESTROY the works of the devil, even in the beginning promised His children not only salvation for the soul, but healing for the body. He did not leave man to wander around in the darkness of the sinful life he had chosen, but, recognizing that darkness, and seeing man's condition, He offered him a way out. There was a way out; but there was only one way out. There is a way out today, but there is only ONE way out. There is ONE way; there is ONE door; there is ONE balm in Gilead; and all other ways will prove futile and vain. Praise the Lord, some of us have found that way. Found the Way so surely that it is the most real thing in our lives and what is more blessed that to tell others the great eternal truth,

"I was lost; but Jesus found me
    Found the sheep that went astray
Threw His loving arms around me,
    Drew me back into His WAY."

In the book of Exodus, wherein we read the story of the deliverance, marvelous, supernatural and complete, of the children of Israel from the bondage of Egypt, we find that God made a certain covenant with His people. They had been murmuring because of the Marah waters of bitterness they had found on their journey had failed to live up to the test imposed upon them by God. After turning the bitter waters into sweet and teaching the Israelites a lesson in the power of faith, He who furnished the pillar of cloud by day and the pillar of fire by night made a promise to, and a covenant with, His people. "If thou wilt diligently hearken to the voice of the Lord thy God and wilt do that which is right in His sight and wilt give ear to His commandments and keep His Statutes, I will put none of these diseases upon thee which I have brought upon the Egyptians, FOR I AM THE LORD THAT HEALETH THEE." (Exodus 15:26)

This promise of healing was not to a wayward people. This promise was given to a people who would meet that opening word "if" face to face and measure up to the standard that God demanded. And when they measured up to the precept God fulfilled the promise. But here you will clearly see the relationship between salvation and divine healing.

We find in this same journey sickness came upon Miriam, the sister of Moses, because of the sin of backbiting and criticizing her brother. Leprosy seized upon the woman whose timbrel had sounded in bygone days over Egypt's dark sea, and whose voice had chanted the praises of the Lord. Sin and sickness took hold upon her together and there was no bodily healing for her until atonement for sin had been made. In the extremity of his trouble Moses cried unto the Lord, "Heal her now, O God, I beseech Thee," and God heard the cry and the deliverance of Miriam came when she had accomplished the atonement for her sin as prescribed by the Lord.

So it ever will be found. The promises for healing are not to a wicked and iniquitous generation, but to the people who have found a personal Savior; and, knowing His power to save, are convinced of His might to heal. Our hearts have thrilled as we have read that the prophet of old who championed the cause of God on the summit of Carmel healed the sick and even raised the dead, and when the mantle of Elijah fell upon Elisha, in the name of the Lord the healings continued. From far away Syria came the captain of the King's host, convert of a waiting maid, to draw his chariot before the door of the prophet of God. ONE way was open to him and one way alone. The waters of Damascus would not suffice but the plan of God was worked out in Jordan. Naaman's leprosy departed and his flesh was restored again as the flesh of a little child.

The shepherd boy to manhood grown is ruling over the destiny of Israel. The Lord who fought with him when Goliath of Gath went down to defeat is still abiding in his heart by faith and is still his shield and his buckler. His heart is thrilled as he enumerates the blessings of the Lord and he calls upon his soul to extol the praises of God. "Bless the Lord, O my soul. And all that is within me bless His holy name. Who forgiveth all thine iniquities and who health all thy diseases" (Psalm 103:3). Like a rolling in of the tide on the sands of the sea there comes into the heart of the sweet singer of Israel the billows of the glory of the Lord. From the time he slew the lion and the bear he has felt His leadership and His presence, and now His blessings are to be told and His goodness proclaimed. The first two blessings of which he speaks are salvation and healing. Well might he sing with grateful heart and tuneful voice, "Bless the Lord all His works in all places of His dominion; bless the Lord, O my soul."

Now we come to the prophet of the captivities. Through the darkness of the night he is looking toward the promise of a golden day. In glory and in triumph the deliverer will come. "Break forth into joy; sing together ye waste places of Jerusalem. All the ends of the earth shall see the salvation of our God" (Isaiah 52:9). Then the Christ of the atonement appears to the prophet. He sees

Him in the travail of His soul. He sees the price that must be paid and he cries with true prophetic fervor, "Surely He hath borne our griefs and carried our sorrows (pains); yet we did esteem Him stricken, smitten of God and afflicted. But He was wounded for our transgressions, He was bruised for our iniquities; the chastisement of our peace was upon Him and with His stripes we are healed." Then, as if he could see the burden of the sin and pain and suffering of the whole world laid upon the back of the matchless Man of Galilee, he cried out, "All we like sheep have gone astray; we have every one to his own way; and the Lord hath laid on Him the iniquity of us all" (Isaiah 53:6). When that prophetic telescope was turned down the vista of the ages the prophet saw to the very heart of atonement truth. Not for the kingdom age was salvation and not for the kingdom age was healing; but both were for the sons of men in every day in every clime who would turn to the Lord and live.

But some have raised the objection that the

healing referred to in Isaiah is the healing of the soul and is spiritual, and has no relation whatever to healing for the body. That objection can best be answered by the words of the book itself. In the gospel according to St. Matthew and the 8th chapter you will find recorded the ministry of the healing Christ. In tenderness and love and compassion He had gone about among the people speaking words of cheer and forgiveness and teaching the truths of the kingdom. The day was far spent and evening was coming over the city. Sometimes we can almost see the people as they brought their sick to Jesus. Mothers with their little children, frail and pinched and wan, looking into His eyes and asking the touch of a hand of love. Old men leaning on the arms of their sons asking for a word from the lips of the Man of Galilee, and women old and bent and laden with suffering and care looking appealingly into His eyes. Then we see Him. He stretches forth the hand and the fever is gone. He speaks and at the sound of His voice the cripple leaps for joy and the baby healed from sickness coos and croons in its mother's arms. Tender, loving, forgiving, healing Christ,

"At even when the sun was set,
    The sick, O Lord, around Thee lay;
Oh with what divers pains they met,
    And with what joy they went away."

He healed them all. Praise His name. Glory be unto Him forever and forever. The same Christ walks in our midst today. He speaks and loves and forgives and heals. Jesus of Nazareth passed by.

He healed them all, "That it might be fulfilled which was spoken by Esaias the prophet, saying: 'Himself took our infirmities and bare our sicknesses.'" Here we have Matthew's interpretation of Isaiah 53. Clearly this was healing for the body and not only salvation for the soul. Look up little mother with heart bowed down with weight of you, Jesus is passing your way. Rejoice ye lame and halt and blind for the Great Physician now is near, the sympathizing Jesus. There is a way that leads to your healing, a road that will lead to the sunshine. It winds past the judgment hall of Pilate down by the way of weeping until it comes to the whipping post and the foot of an old rugged cross. What are these stripes that are spoken of in prophecy? What are these healing stripes that will make the soul of man rejoice? What stripes can they be but the stripes that were placed upon His kingly back when they scourged Him at the whipping post? When the cruel Roman soldiers driven on by hate and scorn nailed Him to the cross, He paid then for your iniquities, He atoned for all your sins. Every wrong of your life, every sin of your days He paid for there as He bowed His head and cried and died; but He paid for your sicknesses and pains at the post of scourging, and eventually emerged in triumph from the tomb to offer you a complete and full and free salvation. Sing all ye redeemed of earth, and chant His praises ye angelic throngs; sing and shout for joy; the work is finished, the atonement is complete, Jesus reigns, rules in the throne room of every heart that will receive Him as Savior, Healer, Baptizer, and the Coming King. Oh my brother, my sister, open wide your heart's door to receive Him; despised, rejected of men, Man of Sorrows and acquainted with grief.

"The foxes found rest and the birds their nest
In the shade of the forest tree,
But Thy couch was the sod O Thou Son of
God
On the deserts of Galilee;
But come to my heart, Lord Jesus,
There is room in my heart for Thee."

Clear as the noonday sun is it to all unprejudiced readers of the word that our healing has been provided for, and it must be as equally clear that the way has been shown down which our feet can tread, weary and worn to the enjoyment of the experience. The seventy were sent out by Jesus in the days of the long ago to preach and to heal in the name of the Lord and they returned with great joy because the results far exceed their most hopeful anticipations. The disciples previous to Pentecost taught and healed with the Master, and when at last the Lord had said goodbye and the Ascension had taken place from Olivet they went at His bidding to tarry for the enduement with power from on high. From the glory of that Pentecostal chamber they went as tongues of living fire. Baptized with the Holy Ghost, filled with all the glory of the Lord, preaching, teaching and proclaiming the kingdom of a resurrected Christ, they went from city to city healing the sick that were therein. Philip was found in Samaria holding a model revival meeting, not only preaching the gospel of the Christ he served but obeying that same Master's instructions and praying for the sick. Peter and John introduced another great revival campaign that resulted in the conversion of thousands by bringing deliverance to the lame man in the name of the Lord at the beautiful gate of the temple. The story of the healing, saving Christ was told far and near until the fiery evangelism of Apostolic days had crossed the seas and was spreading with the rapidity of a prairie fire in distant lands. Everywhere the Apostles went and preached, "The Lord worked with them, confirming the Word with signs and wonders following." Some have raised the objection that the gift of healing was given to the disciples to enable them to establish the Christian Church and at the end of the Apostolic period the gifts were taken from the church. All such objectors should be asked one question: "chapter and verse, please?" and you will generally find that a long system of explanation has to be gone into during which no direct scripture passages are given and such passages as occur in the fifth chapter of James are entirely ignored. Here we find a man, the first president of the first council of churches of Christ ever assembled, austere, conservative, dignified James, writing under inspiration telling us in the last chapter of his Epistle to the Jews in the Dispersion that healing was a part of the gospel for them. "Is any among you afflicted, let him pray. Is any merry? Let him sing psalms. Is any sick among you? Let him call for the elders of the church and let them pray over him, anointing him with oil in the name of the Lord and the prayer of faith shall save the sick, and the Lord shall raise him up and if he hath committed sins they shall be forgiven him."

If one man has the right to single out that passage and claim without direct scriptural authority that those verses applied ONLY to Apostolic times or the kingdom age then another has the same right to make the same claim for the whole book of the epistle. Praise be to the Lord, thousands of people all over the country can testify to the fact that Jesus is the same yesterday, today and forever, and that He has not only the power to save, but the power to heal. Wake up, church of the living Christ, and equip yourself with the whole armor of God. Arise, thou that steepest and Christ shall give thee light. Pray through every fog and mist of doubt and unbelief until the promises of God are made real and we begin to believe, once again that the Bible is God's own word, and that His promises are sure and eternal.

The limitations of God's power are the limitations of our own faith; provision HAS been made for the healing of the body and the people whose spiritual eyes have been opened can see a surety that there is ample scriptural authority for our praying for the sick. If there was no direct or indirect reference to the physical body, we still have a multitude of promises upon which to stand in asking for the physical restoration of ourself or another. "Whatsoever ye shall ask in My Name that will I do," and other wonderful golden promises upon which our feet can stand are found in the Word of the Lord we love.

Across the platform in one of our meetings rows of people are coming weary and tired and sick in body to lay their burdens at the feet of a healing Christ. Ten thousand pairs of eyes are watching intently and thousands of hearts are lifted in prayer, for the Arena is filled to overflowing on this night, when we lift our hearts and voices together in prayer for the touch of a divine hand. Older people are prayed for, some of them can be seen crossing the stage with hands uplifted toward heaven and their forms shaking under the sobs of gratitude because they have felt His presence. But we stop, for in front of us is a little girl, curly headed, hopeful, eager, looking into our eyes with her own tear-dimmed orbs, and as we watch her we can see her lips moving in prayer. We are down on our knees now by her side and she watches intently as we ask, "Darling, what is it you want of the Lord?" She looks shyly at us for a moment and answers back, "I want Jesus to heal me, if you please."

"What is your trouble, my dear?" we inquire.

For answer she puts forward one of her little limbs, and then we can see the cruel braces of steel that hold both legs so tight in their iron clasp and notice the frail wasted little limbs that are too weak to stand without support. She reaches for our hands and in a minute we discover that the whole back is enclosed in a system of braces and even over the shoulders does this network of steel and strap have to be placed. With a trembling little voice she informs us that some of these straps never come off, not even at night when her baby prayers have been said and she lays down, tired and weary little frame, to sleep.

We clasp her in our arms for a moment and ask, "Tell me, little sister, do you believe that Jesus will heal you?"

Quick as a flash comes her answer, "Oh, I just know He will, 'cos in the Bible He promised to heal us and mamma says He just loves little children."

I MIGHT have taken her in my arms and said, "No, dear, you are mistaken. He will not heal you. He USED to heal little children in the days of long ago. He USED to make little paralyzed limbs whole again so that little girls like you could run and laugh and play. You see, my poor little girl, he did it in the old days, by the waters of Galilee and the cities of old Judea because He wanted to prove He really was the Son of God. And later, dear, He allowed His disciples to pray for little girls like you so He could start His church off right, you know, but when that was done He took all the power away. No, dear, you must run along and make the best of it. I know there is no hope for you; no physician can help you; the Great Physician USED to help girlies like you but He does not do it anymore. What is that? About the Bible promises? Well now, some day you will understand. You know it TALKS about healing and praying for the sick, but you know it does not really mean it. It DID mean it once, and some men say it MIGHT mean it again; but it does not mean it for you. Hobble along there, now, dear. Make the best of it. Dry those little eyes and someday, perhaps—someday—you might—"

NO! NO! NO! We cannot tell her that. On that desk before us is the Word. Word of the LION of the tribe of Judah. Word of God. Word with power and authority. Word of

Truth. Oh, blessed word, inspired, kept by power divine, light unto our feet and lamp unto our path, we look into thy pages for guidance. Promises divine—page upon page—breathing to YOU and to ME the messages of the Master. Then by our side we feel a presence. His form cannot be seen—His voice cannot be heard. But HE is there—we know Him—we feel HIM. "Jesus, Savior, Healer, Lord, Thou didst heal people in the days of the long ago. We have read Lord how the mothers of 'Salem their children brought to Jesus and we come to Thee, dear Lord, to ask Thee to lay Thine own nail-pierced hand in love and healing power on the body of this little child. Heal her now, dear Lord." Our prayer dies away in a sob, and then we place on the little forehead the oil of anointing and while a silence that is almost oppressive is in the building we command the paralysis to depart in the Name of the Lord Jesus Christ of Nazareth. A little quiver goes through the frame of the child. She sways and then is prostrate under the power. A moment or two later we can hear a little voice, "Jesus, I do love you. You have healed me, Jesus. Thank you, Jesus—oh, thank you—I—love—you, Jesus—I—love—you—" Thousands of people are shouting the praises of the Lord. Thousands of eyes are moist with tears—thousands of hearts are rejoicing. There seems to be emblazoned in letters of red across the portal of every mind:

"JESUS CHRIST: THE SAME: YESTERDAY, TODAY AND FOREVER."

Is it any wonder that the altars are crowded? Is it any wonder that scores of men, sometimes hundreds, are on their knees crying out for salvation? A voice is heard. Just a little mother starting to sing from a heart filled with love and gratitude, "It is just like Jesus."—The audience picks up on the refrain and it rolls like a great organ through the building:

"It's just like Jesus to roll the clouds away,
It's just like Jesus to keep me day by day,
It's just like Jesus all along the way,
It's just like His great love."

CHAPTER 3
HOW TO RECEIVE YOUR HEALING

It has been clearly shown that your healing has been provided for and that we are keeping within the bounds of good scripture teaching when we pray for the sick and ask the Lord to touch the bodies of the infirm and crippled and ailing. No one doubts that the salvation of the soul of every sin-sick son of Adam's race was purchased by the Lord Jesus on Calvary, and the complete work of atonement finished there. But notwithstanding the fact that a man's salvation was purchased by the efficacious sacrifice of Calvary and the vicarious suffering of our Lord, some men are still unsaved and the vast majority of the people of the world have never known the peace of sins forgiven. The reason for this is simple; they have never availed themselves of the privileges of this purchased, but offered salvation. The sacrifice on Calvary only means something to the man who will accept it and its power is lost if we continue to reject it. There is a way of salvation and there is only one way. That way is clearly outlined in the New Testament Word of God and we are taught that if we try to enter the Kingdom of Heaven in any other way we are thieves and robbers. That is the way of receiving Christ as a personal Savior by an act of faith; faith in His Word; faith in His promises; faith in His sacrifice, and faith that the work is done. We sing sometimes in one of our hymns, "He writes the pardon on my heart THE MOMENT I BELIEVE." That line contains the very center of the truth of faith as it applies to conversion. The purchase of your salvation was the part the Savior played in your redemption; the RECEIVING of that salvation BY FAITH and faith alone, is the part you play in your redemption. One would be lost without the other. If it were otherwise you would be mere automata; mechanism moved about on the stageboard of this world's affairs by wires of control held in the hands of God. But you are a free moral agent. You have the power of choice; you can reject or you can accept, and this power places upon YOU the responsibility for your salvation. If a man is lost, he can never blame God for the fact. He is not lost because of a divine judgment half so much as he is lost because of his willful refusal to accept salvation. Man holds inviolate within his own breast the key that will unlock to him his own eternal destiny. When the monk who lit the fires of the reformation brought the light of truth to a darkened world and a corrupt church, the torch that kindled the blaze was the central, cardinal truth of all real Christian experience, justification by FAITH. Without faith it is impossible to please God. Not by works of penance or deeds of philanthropic fervor but by simple faith in the promises of God, was the soul of man to be redeemed from destruction and saved for all eternity. Faith was the one doorway through which we could pass from anticipation to realization. Faith and faith alone was the portal through which our sin-sick, weary souls could travel from hope to possession of the promised land. So it is in the realm of healing. The stripes purchased the healing of the body, for with His stripes we are healed. But faith and faith alone will make that healing real. The Master Himself was getting at the meaning of faith when He said in the days of the long ago, "When you pray, believe that ye receive and ye shall receive." It is not sufficient to ask the Lord for healing; the work is done when we accept it as done.

Some time ago in one of the great campaigns that meant salvation and healing to many thousands of people, a poor man was kneeling at the altar weeping as if his heart would break. There is always something that touches the heart-strings in the sight of a weeping penitent at the mourners' bench, but this man attracted my attention because it was the fifth or sixth time he had been there. Making my way down through the crowded altars I at last arrived at his side and kneeling beside him asked him if he needed help. He turned his tear-dimmed eyes toward me and said:

"Do I need help? I should say I do. Brother, why won't Jesus save me when He saves everybody else around here? That fellow over there just got through hollerin' for joy and the Lord just walks right by me. I can't get saved at all, brother, and I wish you would tell the Lord about me."

"Of course I will," I replied, "but, brother, do you know the reason that the Lord does not save you, is because you will not let Him. Now don't interrupt me; let me explain what I mean. I know what you are after, you are seeking for FEELING. You want an experience like these other people around here who have testified, and who have been shouting the praises of the Lord. I do not blame you for that, but you must know that you cannot feel anything you do not possess. There must be a point of contact somewhere if you are going to feel anything. I have a pencil in my hand. Can you feel it? No! Tell me why you cannot feel it. That's it! to be sure; because you do not have it to feel. I feel it because I have it. Now, brother, listen to me; how in the world can you expect to feel salvation if you do not have it? How can you FEEL Christ if you do not possess Him? Remember, Jesus died to save you. He has done all He can for your redemption. Now let us pray together and ask Him to receive us."

We bowed our heads and prayed. Sentence by sentence he repeated after me the words of a simple prayer in which we promised the Lord we would always serve Him and love Him, and in the prayer, so simple that a child could have understood the words, we accepted Christ as a Savior.

He opened his eyes, and gazed into mine. He did not speak but waited for me to say something, and so I said, "Praise the Lord, brother, you belong to the King."

"Am I a Christian?" he asked incredulously.

"Why, brother, you must believe His word," I said. "Did you not just now take Him as your Savior and did He not promise to save you?"

"Why, He did do that very thing, didn't He," he replied as his eyes opened a little wider. He paused in thought a moment and then he burst enthusiastically out with:

"Say, I AM a Christian, brother. If His word is any good and it is true I AM a Christian, if I died in a minute, would I go to heaven?"

"Surely you would, brother," I told this unchurched man of the street. "He died to save you and you are saved right now."

It was interesting to watch his face as his faith took hold. The realization dawned upon him; his eyes flashed as he repeated to himself softly and musingly, "Saved! Saved right now; a Christian…a real Christian right now!" Then came a veritable explosion. It was THE MOMENT HE REALLY BELIEVED IT, and at that moment it became real.

Doubts were swept away. Unbelief was gone. He took one deep breath and hollered, "Hip, hip, hooray—I mean glory, hallelujah. Praise the Lord."

He was on his feet now and shouting for all he was worth. "Oh, brother, hallelujah; oh glory, glory," until I had to quiet him and ask him to be as still as possible, for other souls were praying through a salvation. I could never understand a salvation without feeling. But salvation to be felt must be possessed, and we can only possess it by faith. Healing to be felt must be possessed, and we can only possess by faith.

COMMON MISTAKES

We have prayed for thousands and thousands of people during the past few months and we say to the glory of God we have seen thousands of people healed from all manner of diseases and sicknesses, but many, many people have been turned away empty because they did not understand. In the opening healing service in the great Vancouver campaign we prayed for twenty-five people. Scores were there who wished to be reached, but there was an evident lack of faith that made us tell them to wait. As the healings were seen night after night the great throngs of people who attended the meetings had their faith grow by leaps and bounds until on the closing day of that meeting we prayed for one-thousand, five-hundred people individually at a single service. As many as one-hundred at a time were prostrate under the power of God, and the faith of the people seemed to be rolling in billows through the great Arena. According to the estimates of the Patrick brothers, who owned the building, over a quarter of a million people heard the word of God in that Armenian the space of three weeks. The city was shaken, and the testimonies of healing came in from every hand and side.

It is impossible to reach multitudes of people like that without knowing WHY some are healed and some people are not. In this chapter we want to deal with some of the common mistakes and then show clearly how we should approach the Lord in asking for healing for the body. The first mistake is a very common one. DO NOT BELIEVE THAT THE MAN WHO PRAYS HAS ANY SPECIAL HEALING POWER OR VIRTUE. The one who prays for you is not your healer. Just a sinner saved by grace; just a brand snatched from the eternal burning; nothing but a poor halting creature of time touched by the hand of God. No man on earth is WORTHY even to pray for you; no one should ever lay the oil of anointing on your head who does not feel unworthy even to touch the hem of His garment. Get your eyes away from an evangelist or minister or worker and try to focus the eyes of your soul upon the blessed form of one who hung on a rugged cross, and who died to save you there. When people crowd upon us and ask for the touch of our hands, instinctively we feel like drawing away and saying, "Not our hands, sister, but His; not our touch, brother, but the touch of a nail-pierced hand alone can bring you relief." Our hearts have bled as we have seen them come, weary and tired and sad. People who have given up hope, and in whose eyes hope is finding place again. Mothers with their crippled children and men who are leading the blind. Scores of them, hundreds of them, sometimes thousands of them; sick and helpless, maimed and deaf and blind. We have heard them sing,

"The Great Physician now is near,
   The sympathizing Jesus.
He speaks the drooping heart to cheer.
   Oh hear the voice of Jesus,"

and the tears have flowed freely down our cheeks and in our helplessness we have cried out unto the Lord. Only Jesus can heal. Only Jesus can save. Only Jesus can hear and answer that prayer, coming from a broken heart. Then our hearts have thrilled as we have heard the great crowds sing; sing in the fullness of their joy; sing in the gladness of their hearts. And why should they not sing? For have not these same people received the touch of a loving hand? Have not these weary lives been blessed by the Man of Galilee? Have not these burdens been lifted and these sorrows rolled away? Aye, sing on, ye blessed happy pilgrims; sing on and chant your hymns of praise. Sing until the notes that leave your lips roll over the battlements of glory and lodge near a throne of alabaster white in the realms of eternal day. Sing until your hearts are filled with praise and the morning stars shout with you for joy,

"Oh, it is Jesus. Yes, it is Jesus.
Yes, it is Jesus in my soul,
For I have touched the hem of His garment
And His blood has made me whole."

Remember, then, not the one who prays for you, but the ONE to whom he prays is the source of your healing and strength. Glory and praise and dominion and power be ascribed unto His matchless name, forever and forever, world without end. Amen and Amen.

The second mistake that people make is very often found. DO NOT MISTAKE ANXIETY FOR FAITH. Over-anxiety is always an impediment to faith. Anticipation and hope may be stepping-stones that will bring you nearer to the goal of your desire, but to be overly anxious is to fasten a weight around your ankle that will not let you climb. People sometimes come rushing to the meetings and demand to be prayed for immediately, and show signs of aggravation when you ask them to with their turn and make the spiritual preparation that we feel is necessary. Of course, everybody who is sick is anxious to be healed. That is perfectly natural, but there is nothin in that anxiety to heal you or to bring you relief. So many times we have seen a look of disappointment on the faces of the people when there should have been the sign of the happiness and joy because they made the mistake of coming to receive their healing, indeed being anxious to receive it, when as a matter of face they did not know how. People who have never served the Lord a day in their lives crowd to the front; people who have never attended a prayer meeting in years and who hear on Sunday the call of the open road rather than the pealing of the church bells will ask for healing, with no thought of a real consecration of the life to God and of days of service lived in His name. Let your consecration be deep and sincere. Let your life be filled with His praise, and let your hearts be full to overflowing with His love. When people realize that the preparation for healing is always spiritual, and that they are really nearer their healing when they believe that the healing of the soul is of more importance after all than the healing of the body, they are coming nearer and nearer to the possession of that faith that will mean the end of their troubles and the beginning of a brighter and better day.

Intellectual assent is not faith. The assent of the mind might be necessary to faith, but the power of appropriation must be added to it before it can become real living faith. Mental concentration is not faith; the mere statement that you believe does not necessarily mean that you really do. Struggling with mental powers and faculties will never bring it, for faith IS A GIFT OF GOD. It will never be imparted by God until the spiritual condition of the believer warrants the gift. By this we must not believe that the believer must have attained to a certain condition of piety or have lived for so many days or years a certain high type of life, for we read in the Word of sinners having great faith in the days of Jesus, so much so that the Master Himself commented on the power of their faith. No matter what the past has been, the faith was there because the spiritual intent at the moment of their petition was away from self, the flesh and the world are directed only toward heaven and God. We have seen men from the streets, broken and contrite before the altars of penitence, weeping their way through to the cross on which the Prince of Glory died, receive that self-same night miraculous healing for the body. In one of the campaigns held in a certain large town an unusual altar call had been given and hundreds of people had made their way to the mourners' benches and in the old-fashioned way were pouring out their hearts to the Lord. Society people from the larger homes of the city were kneeling side by side with the ill-clad inhabitants of the East Side and mingling their prayers and their tears as they sought the forgiveness of a tender and merciful Christ. When the altar call was nearly over and already small groups of people were singing hymns of joy and salvation, as an usher called our attention to the figure of a man walking down the aisle. He was well dressed and looked prosperous, but the way his frame was bent told of a sorrow or trouble in his life. The usher whispered in our ears, "I do not believe that man has been to church for twenty years. Everybody knows him here… poor fellow…they knew his trouble. For ten years he has been an inveterate dope fiend; he is the worst slave in this town. If that man is converted, it will shake this town."

We watched him as he slowly marched down the aisle. We could see he was struggling within himself as he halted for a brief moment at the altar. Then on his knees he went and buried his face in his hands. Quietly we knelt at his side. He needed no helper; he was engaged in prayer.

"Jesus...I am no worthy...I have sinned, and I come to Thee tonight, Lord, for the first time in years...I believe thou are the Christ...I believe, Lord...I believe. Jesus...Jesus. Can you save a...a...SLAVE?"

He opened his eyes and looked into ours. We felt led to speak: "Him that cometh unto Me I will in no wise cast out."

Five minutes passed and the great audience was on its feet singing with one accord and form the fullness of thousands of hearts, "Jesus breaks every fetter, and He sets me free." But down at the altar one man was still kneeling, his eyes closed, his hands clasped and his lis moving in prayer.

"I will shout hallelujah, for He sets me

free," sang the audience as the rafters trembled under the volume of song and the strains floated through the open windows and out on to the streets. At the altar a man was praying He alone of these thousands was on his knees, hands clasped, head bowed, eye closed in prayer. "There is rest for the weary, there is rest for you," sang out the congregation until it seemed that the very building itself was filled with the presence of the glory of the Lord and our hearts would break with the joy of it all.

At the altar a man was praying: "A slave, Jesus; just a slave, Jesus…a slave…but you promised…promised, Jesus…you promised SLAVES like me that you would…"

"On the other side of Jordan,
Where the tree of life is blooming,
There is rest for the weary,
There is rest for you."

thundered the audience, until the last echoes of the song had died away and the benediction was falling upon ears that that night had heard of the power of the Lord. Outside the street car bells were ringing. Crowds were surging, automobile horns were tooting, and once in a while the strains of a hymn came floating back to the building. Listen! we can hear it…"Jesus breaks every fetter and He sets me free."

They are singing on the street car going home, and the people in the motor cars take up the refrain. At the altar a man is kneeling, eyes closed, head bowed, hands clasped in prayer. "Only a slave, Jesus…only a slave… but you promised, Jesus…that you would save…unto the uttermost…"

Down the aisle there came one who wore a seamless robe in the days that have long sped by, and we are told that before He was born in Bethlehem of Judea the angel said His name should be called Jesus, "for He shall save His people from their sins."

"Only a slave, Lord Jesus…but you promised…" Down the aisle came the Man of Sorrows, who knew, who understood, who loved and who cared. No eye could see Him, no ear could catch the tread of His feet. But He stopped, just as He stopped at the cry of blind Bartimaeus on the Jericho highway, and listened.

At the altar a man was praying... praying..."Just a slave, Jesus...helpless... weak..."

A moment later in a city far beyond the stars, where the streets are paved with gold and the walls are of jasper, the bells were pealing...pealing, pealing and the choirs were singing...singing...singing...for a soul...a slave...had been redeemed and they were glad.

At the altar a man was standing. His arms were outstretched toward heaven; his eyes were open and lit with the radiance of heaven's own joy; his face was aglow with a glory that was divine. He was praying, "A slave, Lord Jesus, and you rescued me...a slave, and now I am free, Jesus...Oh, Jesus... Glory...glory...glory, Lord..." and through the open window we could hear them singing as the cars pulled out, "Jesus breaks every fetter, and He sets me free."

Healed of the dope habit. Chains broken; shackles smashed; barriers torn away; saved and healed by power divine.

A man is standing at the altar. He is in a large church listening to the words of the preacher: "I give you then the right hand of fellowship and welcome you in to the communion of this church. May God richly bless you, my brother…and make this church a blessing to you." The congregation breathes a fervent "Amen." The man turns from the altar; head erect; eyes tear-dimmed but filled with happiness and joy; he USED to be a slave…just a slave…until he met JESUS. Jesus, Savior, healer, breaks EVERY fetter… and He sets me free.

So we find in coming for our healing that it is not because of our righteousness or our church membership, or our deeds of Christian charity and love, that we can lay claim to the promise of the Lord, but it is because at that moment we give ourselves unreservedly to Him; to His promise and to His Word and take our healing from Him in simple faith. We have found that a broken spirit and a contrite heart and a feeling of unworthiness is generally an assurance of faith enough for healing, while on the other hand many people lose the blessing because they feel they are entitled to it.

THE ATTITUDE YOU SHOULD TAKE

when coming to the Lord for the healing of the body is one of a faith in which all the elements of doubt have been eliminated; the kind of attitude that you should have when you have finished the prayer of supplication and have started the prayer of praise. When a man supplicates, it proves that he does not possess the thing for which he asks. When a man follows the supplicatory prayer by the utterance of praise it proves that he "believes that he receives" the thing for which he asks. It seems to us that a feeling of anticipation and joy would be noticeable on the face of the man who KNEW with believing faith (and that is the kind you must have) that his cancer or his rheumatism was to melt away in a few moments under the touch of the Lord. It is good to ask; blessed it is to petition, but the benediction falls when you receive. There are two kinds of faith: passive faith and active faith. Passive faith says, "I believe Jesus can heal me; I believe Jesus has healed others; the work is possible; I believe that with all my heart." Active faith says, "I believe Jesus can heal, and praise the Lord I AM NOW HEALED. The promise is mine. I take it and I NOW POSSESS IT." Let us illustrate.

A little girl is on the platform, standing before the pulpit, eager and anxious for the prayer of faith. It is very evident that she has been crying, but the tears have been wiped away and a smile is on the little countenance.

"How old are you, little sweetheart?"

"I'm seven, sir."

"Do you love Jesus? I'm sure you must, for you know Jesus loves little children. Tell me dear, what is your trouble?" Her answer is a very pained expression of the face, as she slowly lifts her limb and shows us a very bad crippled and deformed little foot encased in a special large and bulky shoe. Under her arm she is holding something that she seems to value, wrapped in a piece of newspaper, and it strikes us as peculiar that she should be carrying such a package on to the platform.

"What have you in the parcel little girl?" Her answer was the change from the expression of pain to a sweet smile. Slowly, in full view of the audience, she unfastened the string and unrolled the paper and to our astonished eyes she presented a new…SHOE. She held it up very proudly and then quietly exclaimed, "I brought it with me so I could wear it home." FAITH! FAITH! FAITH! Unsullied, unspoiled, untarnished by the ravages of a so-called rationalism that is nothing more nor less than gross unbelief masquerading as higher criticism, that faith of a little child reached out and stood upon the promises. Sweet, simple, childlike faith; her Master had spoken, and she believed. "Except ye become converted and become as little children ye cannot enter the kingdom of heaven." We took that shoe and looked at it, and then our eyes turned back to the little girl. Her hands, now freed, were being slowly raised to heaven and her little lips were moving in prayer. We placed upon her forehead the oil of anointment and prayed to the friend of little children and said as we finished, "My little sister, receive your healing in the name of Jesus." No expression of ecstatic joy left her lips. No shout of glory, no word of praise. No exuberance of feeling, no outburst of emotionalism; she just looked at us and smiled. "God bless you, little sweetheart," we said, as we handed her back her shoe. She took it and very deliberately walked over to the chair we have vacated and, stooping over, began to unfasten the shoe on her crippled foot. People gazed at her in amazement. Once she looked up and smiled. Then with a quick jerk off came the shoe and as she placed it by the side of the chair she said, "I won't need that any more, will I?"

She NEVER PUT THAT OLD SHOE BACK ON AGAIN. When she walked off the stage it was with her new shoe on the foot that had been crippled.

"Who healed you, dear?"

"Jesus."

She walked to the end of the platform, stopped a moment and then went on again, saying as she went, "Somebody throw that old shoe away; I won't want it anymore."

Out in the audience the people were sobbing. Strong men who came to criticize stayed to pray and women whose lives had been centered in self waited to kneel at the feet of the friendless prisoner of Pilate's judgment hall and tell Him they would serve and love Him the rest of their lives. The little child who should lead them had taught a great audience the difference between passive and active faith.

CHAPTER 4
HOW TO KEEP YOUR HEALING

The question is often asked: "Is it possible to lose your healing after once the touch of a loving Savior's hand has been laid upon your head, or the divine voice has spoken to you telling you that you are made whole?"

To this question there is but one answer, and that is that it is possible for you to lose your healing and to sink back again into the state, both spiritually and physically, that the Lord by His grace has lifted you from.

Let us turn tonight to the fifth chapter of the Gospel according to Saint John, and there we shall find the story of the man who was healed by Jesus by the side of the pool called

Bethesda.

In the story we are told that there was a feast of the Jews held in the city of Jerusalem. In all probability this was the Feast of the Passover, and Jesus had gone to the city to be with His disciples and undoubtedly to minister to the waiting multitudes.

Close by the sheep market was the pool whose waters were troubled at certain periods by the touch of an angel. And around the edge of the pool a waiting multitude of sick and impotent folk had gathered, waiting for the angel touch.

It is not significant that this pool, called Bethesda, meaning the place of mercy, was near by the busy mart of human industry, the sheep market, and that Jesus was found in the place where He was needed?

Not only in the busy marts of human industry; not only in the stately cathedrals; not only in the village chapel, or among a great concourse of people such as we have tonight, is Jesus Christ found, but wherever there is the cry of a hungry heart, wherever there is a sob of distress, wherever there is the need for the touch of a Savior's hand, there we find Jesus.

And so it was that Jesus passed by the pool that was the place of mercy, and saw there an impotent man who had an infirmity thirty and eight years.

In tenderest love and compassion the eyes of the Master were focused upon him, and Jesus seemed to see through the rough exterior down to the very intent of his heart. He knew that the man that had been suffering for thirty-eight years could not find help in any power but the one the Master possessed. Because He saw the need, and knew that He had power to meet that need, He said to the man, "Wilt thou be made whole?"

Oh friends, weary and sin-sick, heavily laden with the cares and toils of a weary world, "Wilt thou be made whole?"

Oh brother of mine, suffering the pains of disease and knowing the gnawing of corruption in that body of yours, don't you hear, too, the voice of the Nazarene, "Wilt thou be made whole?"

And you, little mother, so busy and distressed with the cares of the home and the children, looking and longing through the darkness of your night for the dawning of a happy day, "Wilt thou be made whole?"

And you, too, little children, with your limbs enclosed in the cruel case of steel, and your voices hushed because of the pain in your little bodies, "Wilt thou be made whole?"

Jesus, tender, loving, sympathetic Man of Galilee, is standing by your side and, looking into your eyes, is asking you directly this one question, "Wilt thou be made whole?"

The impotent man gazed into the face of Jesus, and not understanding at first the intent of His question, said unto Him, "Sir, I have no man, when the water is troubled, to put me into the pool; but while I am coming, another steppers down before me."

We do not always understand the intent of the question of Jesus; we do not always grasp the meaning of His Word; we do not always know the depth of divine truth that is contained in the precious Book—the Word of God—but we do not know that, notwithstanding our weaknesses and our misunderstandings and our lack of knowledge, Jesus is willing to help.

Jesus turned to him and said, "Rise, take up thy bad and walk."

I would that everybody in this building tonight could know that Jesus came to break every fetter and to set every prisoner free! To understand that the Lion of the Tribe of Judah shall break every chain and give us the victory, glorious, wonderful, eternal victory, again and again!

I would that you could understand that He came to give you sunshine for your shadow, the oil of joy for mourning, and beauty for ashes here!

Some time ago in a land across the sea, an evangelist was conducting a revival meeting, and the power of God had descended and numbers of people were finding the Christ as a personal Savior. On a memorable Saturday night the evangelist was to preach on the story of the prodigal son, and requested a certain soprano singer in his choir to sing the old hymn, "Where Is My Wandering Boy Tonight?"

She looked into the eyes of the evangelist and said, "Sir, I cannot sing that hymn! Any hymn will do but that. I would love, sir, to sing, but I am afraid it is impossible."

"Why have you an aversion to that particular hymn?" he asked.

With eyes downcast, for a moment she looked as if she were about to cry, when suddenly she raised her head, and as if she had made up her mind to dig up some hidden sorrow, looking into his face she said:

"Fourteen years ago my husband died and my only boy, who was then fourteen years of age, thinking that his earnings should not be given up solely to his mother, burst into a fit of temper one afternoon and left the house; from that day to this I have never even heard of him."

Tears glistened in her eyes, and her bosom heaved convulsively as she continued, "O, sir, is it any wonder when the strains of that hymn come to my ears that my heart is almost broken? I could not sing, sir, I would have to break down. That song would end in a sob."

"But, madam," said the evangelist, "I want you to sing that hymn. That is my subject tonight. You will sing it with a heart filled with feeling and love, and perhaps the Master will bless it to the salvation of some soul."

The night came on apace and found the Church crammed to the doors with people sitting in the window seats, the aisles filled, and every nook and cranny of the building crowded to suffocation.

That evangelist rose in his pulpit, gave out his text, and told the story of how the father welcomed home the returning prodigal. At the conclusion of the sermon, just before that most sacred of all moments the altar call, the soprano singer rose to her feet and commenced to sing with a clear, ringing voice:

"Where is my wand'ring boy tonight—
The boy of my tenderest care,

The boy that was once my joy and light,
The boy of his mother's prayer?"

She struggled bravely through that verse, but in the chorus she broke down once. Something caught in her throat, but she choked it back and then caught up the refrain and carried to the end. By the time she reached the second verse her body was shaking with her sobbing, but she managed to struggle through:

"Once he was pure as morning dew,
As he played at his mother's knee;
No face was so bright, no heart more true,
And none was as gay as he."

Again bravely she went through the chorus with streaming eyes until at last the climax of her emotion and prayer was reached in the words:

"Go for my wand'ring boy tonight;
Go, search for him where you will;

But bring him to me with all his blight,
And tell him I love him still."

From the back of the building a young man arose to his feet, clothed in rags and tatters. Slowly he made his way down the center aisle of the building. Every eye was focused upon the stranger.

A moment or two later he was at the altar; but he passed it by. Then mounting the old-fashioned steps that led to the old-fashioned choir rostrum he fell on his knees at the feet of the woman, and with a voice that could be heard all through the building he cried:

"Mother, you don't mean it do you? Mother, oh mother, you don't mean it!"

She looked into the eyes that she had loved in the bygone days, and a cry of gratitude ascended to God. Then together they made their way down the steps, and kneeling in front of the altar, told the Sinner's Friend the story of a contrite heart, and salvation came into the should of her boy that night.

Did she mean it? Were the words of her

song true? Ah, yes, my friend! You who have known the power of a mother's love know that in spite of the blight and the taint and the sin, his mother loved him still.

Let me say here that you people who know the love of a Christ know also that in spite of the taint and the blight and the sin he loves you still.

The one burning message that I would like to bring into every one of your hearts tonight, the story that I would like to inscribe indelibly upon the tablet of your mind, is the story that Jesus loves you. In spite of the scars. In spite of the wounds, in spite of your sins, Jesus loves you.

Does it not bring hope to your heart and encouragement to your soul to know that in your condition you who sit in this building tonight have a lover in Jesus Christ, one who sympathizes with you, one who understands you, who knows all about you and who loves you with a love that was so deep and strong that it sent Him to the Cross in your place?

You people are tonight by the side of the

pool called Bethesda. You are by the "Waters of Mercy" waiting for the touch of an angel hand and the stirring of the pool. But as you wait let me remind you that Jesus is looking into your eyes and saying, as He did to the impotent man, and to blind Bartimaeus, by the highway side begging, "What wilt thou—what wilt thou—what wilt thou that I should do unto thee?"

Then as you gaze into His eyes, and faith takes hold of your heart and doubts vanish like the night before the dawning of the day, comes the promise of the Lord, "My grace is sufficient for thee; rise, take up thy bad and walk. In my strength shalt thou go out to walk in newness of life."

And so it was that healing came to the impotent man. There was a group of people in the world of that day, just as there is in the world of today, who are very ready to criticize, and they immediately started to destroy the faith of the man who was made whole, and tried to undermine the foundation of faith upon which he had placed his feet.

Is is easy to find fault, and anybody can criticize, but I have never been able to understand the fault finding and criticism that is sometimes offered in the face of a work that is self-evident. When people are healed, and you can see that they are healed and are standing before you, it is inconceivable to believe that sometimes people will say they doubt divine healing and believe that Jesus only healed in the days of the long ago.

If a thing is self-evident it must be a fact. The thing we can see with our eyes is the thing that we must believe. Jesus always brings sufficient proof to any inquiring heart as to the truthfulness of His statements and the integrity of His Word, if only we ask and seek and knock.

In the days of Jesus people criticized because the healing occurred on the Sabbath day. In these days people criticize because healing occur on any day, even though they are just as evident as the healing of this impotent man.

The Healer is the same. His love and truth

and power is the same. And why should not Jesus of Nazareth walk the streets of your city with the same love and tenderness and compassion in His heart as He walked the hills of Judea and the streets of Jerusalem in the days of the long ago?

There is a verse that I want to draw your attention to that contains a thought that should burn itself into the soul of every man and woman who comes to this platform for healing, or who is contemplating kneeling before the Lord and asking for the touch of His hand. That is a statement contained in verse fourteen when Jesus found the healed man in the temple and said unto him, "Behold, thou art made whole; sin no more, lest a worse thing come unto thee."

In this passage we find the truth that inasmuch as a man can obtain his healing, he can also lose it. I believe that if we go back into the realms of sin, and if we deviate from that paths of righteousness, we can lose our healing and perhaps the last condition of our bodies will be worse than the first.

As "we walk in the light, as He is in the light, we have fellowship one with another, and the Blood of Jesus Christ, God Son, cleanseth us from all sin." As we walk in the light of truth, and fasten all our hopes upon Jesus, and keep our affections centered around an old rugged Cross, and maintain an active faith in God's promise and Word, do we keep our healing.

I could recite many stories to you tonight of people who have lost their healing who could have maintained it. It is true that they are very few in number and that the vast majority of the people who are prayed for in these meetings keep their bodily healing. But oh, I would warn you tonight against going back to the flesh pots of Egypt and to the sins of the old life, when before you are the hills and vales, the mountains and glades, and the rivers of the land that flow with milk and honey.

Let me say in conclusion that the man departed and told everybody that he met, that it was Jesus who healed him, and by the word of his testimony he made the praises of the Galilean ring far and wide. We are told in the Scripture that we overcome by the Blood of the Lamb and the word of our testimony. It seems to me to be a mark of ingratitude for people never to tell the story of the Great Physician when they have experienced healing, or to tell of the glory of the Savior when they have known what it is to be saved. It seems to me that sometimes the very stones would cry out the glory of the Lord when our hearts are closed and our lips are silent, and we take God's benefactions and blessings in such a matter-of-fact way. O that we could get the spirit of the Psalmist who, with his heart bursting with a radiance of heavenly joy and his countenance lit with a glow of a light that shone from within, exclaimed, "Oh that men would praise the Lord for His goodness, and for His wonderful works to the children of men!"

"Glory be to Jesus, let the Hallelujah roll,
Help me sing my Savior's praises far and wide,

For I've opened up toward Heaven all the
    windows of my soul,
And I'm living on the Hallelujah side."

Testimony is a messenger of God to hearts that today might be like yours once were. Testimony is a key that will open the door for aching, weary feet to see a path that will lead to a better day. Testimony is a herald that will proclaim the story of a Cross to a world that is heavily laden and worn. Testimony may be the road that will lead to the healing of a weary, pain-racked body and a life that is filled with the darkness of suffering and woe.

Ah, my friends, you remember the lepers: only one returned to give thanks unto the Lord. "Were there not ten cleansed? But where are the nine?" When you come to this platform, or by the side of your own bed you pray for the touch of the Master's hand, look up to Him and in believing faith receive. Then radiant with the joy of salvation, happy in the experience of a healed body, go out to let your light shine before men and to tell the story of a Christ who died to save you.

You say it is a cross? Bear it; and under the Master's guidance the cross of wood will turn to a crown of gold and the burden will change to a ministry of joy.

"I will cherish the old, rugged Cross,
    Till my trophies at last I lay down;
I will cling to the old, rugged Cross,
    And exchange it someday for a crown."

CHAPTER 5
THE JERICHO ROAD

(This sermon stenographically reported.)

You will find the text for tonight in the 18th chapter of the Gospel according to St. Luke. I shall begin to read at the 35th verse and read to the end of the chapter.

We have in this remarkable story an account of the healing of a blind man by the matchless man of Galilee as he happened to come upon him on the Jericho road that day. I want you to notice that it was a personal Christ who went into Jericho, and a personal Christ who left Jericho with a great number of people following in His steps. In the days when Jesus was here among men the people followed Him wherever He went in spite of the maledictions of the Pharisees, and the criticism of the Scribes. The common people heard Him gladly, and wherever Jesus of Nazareth was found, great throngs of people were listening to His words and drinking in the power of the message that fell from His lips. It must have been wonderful indeed to have been able to sit at the feet of Jesus; wonderful to have listened to the messages that satisfied every hungry heart, and brought peace and joy and understanding to the lives who had received his teaching.

Unstintingly He gave Himself. No task was too great, no journey too severe, no work too hard; nothing could deter the Son of Man from going on His errands of mercy and His missions of love. If Jesus were to preach in the days in which we live multitudes would still follow in His train. If the old, rugged cross upon which the Prince of Glory died was to be lifted up before the eyes of men the world would discover that it had not lost its magnetism and the irresistible drawing power of Jesus would still be felt in the hearts of the worldly.

On this particular occasion Jesus was leaving the City of Jericho and I presume the crowds were thronging around Him eager for a touch of His hand or to hear the whisper of His voice. How they must have loved Him; how they must have revered Him! Something in their hearts must have told them that verily this was the Son of God and that He had **power on earth to forgive sins and heal disease.**

By the roadside that day Bartimaeus, a poor, blind beggar, was sitting in his filthy rags. Nobody loved him; nobody cared for his soul; just a despised outcast, a beggar, homeless, friendless and forsaken! His blind eyes could not behold the strange sight of the crowds that were thronging the road, but as he heard the steady tread of the feet of the multitude he inquired of the passerby what this strange commotion meant. "What means this eager, anxious throng that moves with busy haste along?" What means this crowd of people that was stirring up the dust of the narrow winding road that led from Jericho to Jerusalem? Poor Bartimaeus! Little did he know that the only One who could help him was coming close to his side. Little did he understand the reason for the gathering of the throng. Let me say here that I do not believe this was one particular case that Jesus, the Son of God, picked out a demonstration of His power to heal. I rather choose to believe that Bartimaeus just **happened to be there** and that if it had been some other beggar, blind and friendless and forsaken, he too would have received healing from the hands of our gracious Lord. "Who is this," cried Bartimaeus, "What means this noise on the Jericho road this day? Why all this strange commotion and the stir of busy treading feet?" "Oh," cried somebody by his side, "Jesus of Nazareth is passing by." The name went into the heart of Bartimaeus like the shot of an arrow from the bow. That name he had heard before; for strange stories of the miraculous power of the Christ had evidently come to the ears of the poor blind man.

Somebody had told him undoubtedly that away in the north country, by the rolling tumbling waters of Galilee, Jesus had healed the sick and spoken peace to other troubled hearts! There was a logic in the reasoning that went through the mind of the poor blind man as he said within himself, **"What He has done for others He can surely do for me.** If He loved others enough to heal their broken bodies and to open their blinded eyes, will He not do the same for poor blind Bartimaeus? If He has brought joy into the lives of others will He not do the same for me?" In a flash that thought went through his mind. Into the darkened night of this poor beggar's soul, there came just the gleam of starlight. It was not the sun in the meridian height, beaming upon him its full glory and power and majesty. It was merely the shining of a ray through the darkness of the night that had enveloped him. Just a little ray of hope, but, oh, the joy it gave! Hallelujah!

If Bartimaeus had kept his peace, if no cry had been heard proceeding from his lips, this story would never have been told and the healing of this blind man would have never been recorded. But Bartimaeus was wise enough to **walk in the light he had.** I would not call it faith that entered his heart at the moment he heard that Jesus of Nazareth was passing by. I would rather say that a ray of hope flooded the darkened recesses of his soul. Suddenly a cry could be heard ringing sharp and clear through the air,—a cry that must have sounded above the noise and hubbub; a cry that reached the heart of Christ Himself,—busy though He was, leading and teaching the multitude. Sometimes I have heard that cry! I have heard it as I have thought of the story that I now relate and have endeavored to picture the scene on the Jericho road that day. And then again I have heard it in the meetings when some poor wayward wandering sinner had come, sick and weary and searching for the Savior.

"Jesus!" How the name rang out. "Jesus!" Listen to the appeal in it, the throb in it, the petition in it. "Jesus, Thou Son of David, have mercy on me!" Oh, brother of mine, if you forget everything else I have told you tonight, let this thought settle deeply into your consciousness, that no man ever utters that cry but what it is heard by the Man of Galilee. No soul ever cries out to the Lord like that and finds that the Lord turns a deaf ear to that piteous entreaty. Cannot you hear it tonight? Perhaps it is sounding in your own heart at the moment in which I speak. "Jesus, Thou Son of David, have mercy on me."

The multitude thronged around the crying blind man and to the best of their ability endeavored to stifle his appeal. "Why, Bartimaeus, He will never stop for you! The best of the citizens of Jericho are traveling with Him this day. The elite of Jerusalem are following in His steps. He has stopped for others, but He will never stop for you. You are too degraded, too depraved, too low, too despicable! He will pass you by, Bartimaeus. Stop that noise. Let that racket cease, Bartimaeus!"

Oh, the persistency of the cry of the blind

man. The rebukes of the crowd could not stop him. The criticism of the scornful could not deter him. **Jesus was passing by** and that was **enough for blind Bartimaeus.** Louder and louder came his call, and then as if gathering final appeal, he shouted again. "Jesus, Thou Son of David, have mercy on me!"

Then occurred the three sweetest words in the whole of this wonderful incident. The three words that you find at the opening of the 40th verse. **"And Jesus stood."** Yes, praise His name, He stood for a poor blind beggar and one day He stood for me. He stood listening eagerly to the call that came from the heart of that man on the Jericho road. He stood in the days of long ago whenever a cry went from a heart that was broken or emaciated for a life that was distressed and He will stand today. The motto of this campaign is "Jesus Christ, the same yesterday, and today and forever." He never changes. As He sympathized with and loved the poor blind beggar on the Jericho road so

He sympathizes with and loves the people who need Him in the day in which we live. To be robbed of your physical eyesight is an awful thing. My heart goes out in pity and sympathy to the people who grope their way through a darkened world, who can never see the beauty of the flowers and who can never know the glory and the majesty of the eternal mountains. Bad as that may be, spiritual blindness is a thousand times worse. Some men have eyes for the world and naught but the world. Some men look to self and to self alone. Some are clothed in the rags of iniquity and, like Bartimaeus of old, sit in the dust and the dirt and the filth that we can too on every hand and side as over life's pilgrimage we travel. It seems to me that if Jesus listened to the cry of the blind man then He will certainly hear the cry of the blind man now. Oh, brother of mine, with your heartaches, your perplexities, your problems, your sins and your woes, do you know that Jesus of Nazareth passes by? Oh, sister of mine, with the crosses of life heavy upon your shoulders and the burdens of life weighting down your back, with a load that is grievous and heavy to be borne, do you know that the great Burden Bearer is traveling on your road tonight? Jesus of Nazareth is passing by, and Jesus stood,— great, glorious, wonderful words. He who holds the oceans in the hollow of His hand. He who stood on the pedestal of His own eternal glory and from His finger tips divine flung out millions of flaming worlds like ours into space. He who put the color in the petals of the rose and the song in the throat of the feathered warbler. Jesus, the Creator of the universe, stood for a poor blind beggar! That is part of the heart of the Gospel. No matter how needy we may be the Bible says, "My God shall supply all your needs." No matter how low we may be the Lord will raise us up. Just as far as the blighting effects of sin can take a man, just that far will the tender loving hand of Jesus of Nazareth reach down to bring him back to the ways of purity and of peace and of joy. So it was that Jesus heard the cry and commanded the poor old beggar to be brought to Him. All eyes were centered now upon the object of the pity and the love of Jesus. Their rebukes were silenced, their criticisms ceased. They approached the blind man and with encouragement in their tone they said, "Be of good cheer, rise, He calleth thee."

Do you get the significance of that statement? Have you ever applied it to your own hearts? How I wish I could come down among you and take every one of you by the hand and say as the messengers of old were commanded by Jesus to say, "Brother of mine, sister of mine, be of good cheer, rose, He calleth thee." That was the message Jesus sent to the poor blind beggar. That is the message He sends to you tonight. That is the appeal of the Gospel, including everybody in this great building. Rise, He calleth thee. No matter your difficulty, rise, He calleth for you. No matter what your problem, rise, He calleth thee. No matter what your heartache, no matter how strong your habit of how deep your sin, rise, **He calleth for you.**

Blind Bartimaeus would have been very foolish if, having had a little ray of hope shining through the darkness of the night into his soul, he had persisted in sitting by the roadside and not obeyed the word of the Lord. If he had not come to Jesus when the Master invited him to come I doubt greatly if Jesus would have gone to him. The Lord gave him the opportunity to approach the Throne of Grace. He invited him to kneel at His blessed feet and Bartimaeus would have been making the greatest and most foolish mistake of his life if he had not obeyed the word of the Lord. Mark you, he was not healed when Christ extended the invitation. He did not receive the blessing merely because Jesus invited him to come. He **obeyed the word of the Lord** and because he obeyed the word of the Lord he ultimately found the desire of his heart. How foolish it is for anyone have heard the gracious invitation to still sit by the roadside in the dirt and the dust and in rags, blind, unable to see or to appreciate any of the beautiful things of life when Jesus has invited you to come. The moment those glad words fell on the ears of poor Bartimaeus, that moment he was stirred into action. Casting aside his filthy gowns, he rose to his feet and **started to follow Jesus,** led undoubtedly by the throng that surrounded him. His sightless eyes were staring vacantly into space. His heart was beating with suppressed excitement. Perhaps he was praying as he came, but the big thing to me is that **he came.** Bartimaeus stopped in the presence of Christ. What a picture! The Son of God, who left the ivory palaces of His Father's Kingdom, who had been co-existent with God the Father and God the Holy Spirit for the very beginning. The Creator of everything beautiful and everything good on the one side and on the other a poor blind beggar.

We do not know whether or not Bartimaeus had been blind all his life or not. We do not know whether of not it was sin that caused him to lose the sight of his eyes or perhaps in might have been some misfortune that had made him go through the days as if the brightest hours were the darkest hours of night. We do know that he was blind. We do know that he needed Jesus. No word of criticism left the lips of the Lord; no unkind cutting sentence left the heart of the Prince of Peace. That was no standing in judgment over the cringing figure at his feet, but just simply a plain, practical and necessary question. **"What wilt thou that I shalt do unto thee?"** Have you ever heard the voice of the Lord saying that to you, my brother? Have you ever heard that voice that is sweet as bells at evening pealing, echo that question through the corridors of your heart? Glory to Jesus!! What is it you want, my brother? Deliverance from the power of the enemy? Rise, he calleth thee. The breaking of the chains of some vile and sinful habit? Listen! The lion of the tribe of Judah is standing near. Do you need the pain and anguish and physical suffering that you have endured during the past to melt like snow before the rising sun? That Man of Galilee is close by your side. Do you need the peace that passeth all understanding to enter your heart and rule in your life? Then let me tell you as the blind man was told in the days gone by, Jesus of Nazareth passeth by. He is calling to you tonight. What wilt thou that I shalt do unto thee? Oh, what will you answer me? Asking you what is the desire of your heart,—what are you going to say to Jesus? The blind man cried, "Lord, that I might receive my sight!" What else could he reply? **That was what he wanted.** That was what he needed. Sometimes people wonder why their prayer requests are not granted. The scripture has promised "My God shall supply all your needs according to His riches and glory by Christ Jesus our Lord." Notice, my friends, it doesn't say **"your wants,"** it says **"your needs."** Sometimes people want things that they do not really need, but one thing I am going to promise you tonight. One thing is sure as that day follows night and that Jesus is coming again. One thing as sure as the eternal hills, sure as the grand and glorious mountains and that is "My God shall supply all your needs." So cannot you hear His voice tonight? What wilt thou that I shalt do unto thee? When blind Bartimaeus asked the question of the Lord, Jesus replied as he always does reply, "Receive thy sight; thy faith hath made thee whole." The joy bells were ringing in the heart of the blind man. The bells of heaven were pealing in his rejoicing soul. Suddenly the scales rolled away. A shout of rejoicing left his lips. It was taken up by the multitude. It echoed and re-echoed along the Jericho road that day. A shout of victory, a shout of triumph, a shout of glory, the blind man could see. Jesus Christ, the carpenter's son, of Nazareth, could do and would do just what He said He would do. "Receive thy sight, they faith hath saved thee."

In conclusion, my friends, let me state that Jesus never fails. Oh, if you knew the tender loving appeal in the heart of the Man that died for you, not one of you among these assembled thousands would turn away from the Son of God. There is not a broken heart in this city that He cannot heal. Not a life, stained and marred and spoiled by sin but what He can redeem it. Not a lost soul but what He can find it. Not a broken body but what He can heal it. Praise the Lord, Jesus of Nazareth is passing by. Look up, sister, cannot you see Him? Reach out, brother, can't you touch Him? I implore you, I entreat you to obey the call of the Master tonight. Rise. Come unto this altar, break away from the old life and the old ways, He is calling for you. Hallelujah!!!

CHAPTER 6
A MODEL REVIVAL

(This sermon stenographically reported.)

I am going to speak to you tonight on the subject "A Model Revival," and you will find that text which I have chosen for the evening sermon in the 8th chapter of the Acts of the Apostles, beginning to read at the 5th verse and reading to the end of the 8th verse.

"Then Phillip went down to the city of Samaria and preached Christ unto them and the people with one accord gave heed unto those things which Phillip spake hearing and seeing the miracles which He did. For unclean spirits crying with loud voice came out of many that were possessed with them, and many taken with palsies and that were lame were healed. And there was great joy in that city."

I believe that too great a significance cannot be attached to the opening word of the text. The little word **"then."** When was it that Phillip went down to Samaria and held the revival meeting that under the mighty power of God stirred the whole of the city? You know the Jews had no dealings with the Samaritans, and it was a particularly hard field in which Phillip labored, but he had received a special qualification for the work that the Lord had called him to do. He had been one of those men who were privileged to walk in the footsteps of Jesus over the hills of old Judea, by the rolling tumbling waters of Galilee as the Master of men went on his errands of mercy and his missions of love. He was there when Jesus opened the eyes of the blind. He was standing close to the side of his Lord when Jesus unstopped the ears of the deaf and his voice had been raised in a shout of victory as the lame man had walked at the command of the Savior. He was one of that group of men who had listened to the Beatitudes falling from the lips of the Lord. He had been trained in a school of religious instruction sitting at the feet of the Matchless Teacher, Jesus Christ of Nazareth the Son of the Living God. What a privilege! What a blessed and a hallowed experience to come into such close contact with the Savior that he loved.

The sands have been washed in the footprints
   Of the stranger on Galilee's shore,
But the voice that subdued the rough billows
   Will be heard in Judea no more.

But the steps of the lone Galilean
   With joy I will follow each day
And the toils of the road will seem nothing
   When I get to the end of the way.

There are many steep hills to climb upward—
   I am often longing for rest—
But He who appointed my pathway
   Knows just what is needful and best.

I know in His word He has promised;
   My strength it should be as my day
And the toils of the road will seem nothing
   When I get to the end of the way.

Phillip had been following in the footsteps of Jesus and he had obeyed the command of the Lord given, both before and after the crucifixion on the cross and the glorious resurrection from the tomb, to tarry at Jerusalem and wait for the promise of the Father, **the baptism of the Holy Spirit.** He had been one of the 120 that gathered in the sanctity of that upper chamber, praying and waiting in obedience to his Lord's command until the Holy Spirit came. His ears heard the sound of a rushing mighty wind. His tongue had spoken a language he had never used before! His heart was filled when the Comforter came and endued him with power from on high.

That word **"then,"** with which I am opening the text tonight is significant of the fact that Phillip had received divine qualifications for his ministry. After Pentecost, after his baptism, after obedience to his Lord, after the waiting in the upper room, after the tongues of living fire, after the sound of the rushing mighty wind, **then** Phillip went down to Samaria. Will you kindly notice, too, that arriving in the city he did what every minister of the Gospel should do,—**preach Christ** unto the people. He might have handed out a few handbills and told of moving pictures that were to be shown in the parish house, or told of the meeting of the men's club on Tuesday night or the ladies' sewing circle that would meet on Thursday. He might have read the church program with a long list of social events to which the wealthy and the cultured and the refined of the city would be invited. No, he did none of that! **He preached Christ** unto the people and therein we find the secret of the successful evangelism of the Disciple Phillip. **He preached Christ.** What a sermon! What a message!! Just Jesus; born of the Virgin, the eternal Son of God, who came into a sin-cursed world of sin and suffering and sorrow and sickness to pay the penalty for all our transgressions on the Cross of Calvary. He told of Jesus who left the ivory palaces of his father's home to appear as a babe in the manger at Bethlehem, to grow to manhood and give Himself without stint and without reserve to the people for whom He died. Have we forgotten the old, old story of the love of the Matchless Man of Galilee in these days of spiritual apostasy? Have we forgotten the tender pleading of the Voice that sounds through our ears and echoes in the corridors of our souls? The Voice that is sweet as bells at evening pealing, "Come unto me all ye that labor and are heavy laden and I will give you rest." Do you not remember the words of the Master, "And I, if I be lifted up will draw all men unto me!" The world will never be saved and sin will never find redemption by the preaching of community uplift and lecturing on social reform. What the heart of the sinner needs is not a discourse on the housing problem or some lecture on the subject of labor and capital; the sinner needs the Gospel for the Gospel alone can save. It is not sufficient to preach the teachings of Jesus. Jesus was not a teacher; **he was a Savior.** He is not the way-shower—**he is the Way!** He is not the revealer of light—he said, **"I am the light."** He is not the importer of truth, **he is the truth.** Our only hope of heaven, our only gateway to glory! Hallelujah! There is no mistaking the definite, clear, concise statement of the Lord, "No man cometh unto the Father but by Me." Yes, praise the Lord, he **preached Christ** unto the people and because there was a power in the message and an all sufficiency in the Gospel that he delivered, wonderful results attended his ministry and Samaria was stirred from center to circumference. The preaching of "Jesus and Him crucified" will bring the same result in the day in which we live as the same message brought in the days of long ago. The power is in the message, not in the messenger. The power is in the Gospel, not in the man that preaches it and no man can ever enjoy the inspiration and the power and the presence of the Holy Ghost who does not preach the Gospel!

Phillip not only preached the Gospel to the people but he evidently held healing services for the sick, for we read in the 6th verse that the people with one accord gave heed unto the things that he said because they saw the miracles that he performed. Sometimes objectors have said we should not pray for the sick in public. It is too great a spectacle and means too much excitement in the services, we learn. It is very evident that in this particular instance Phillip preached Christ unto the people, and in conjunction with his preaching ministry he enjoyed a healing ministry as well for the people **heard** and **saw** the miracles which he did. How in the world could they see them if he prayed for the sick in some back room as if he was ashamed of the power of God? How in the world could they have heard the dumb speaking if Phillip had laid on hands and anointed with oil in some dark corner away from the gaze of the assembled multitude as if the people for whom he prayed were ashamed of the Great Physician? No, **right out in the open** where the eyes of the incredulous could see! Where the skeptics could behold! Where the scoffers could know! Phillip prayed for the sick and because the Lord was in the Gospel that he preached the sick were wonderfully and marvelously healed. We have no apology to make for our method of reaching the people. In the days of Jesus Himself He prayed for the sick in the synagogues; in the open air wherever opportunity offered, and because of the healing of Jesus many came to follow Him and to know Him as a Savior.

Divine healing is the heritage of every real Christian and belongs to every man and woman that will give themselves to the Lord and enjoy a real born again experience. I want you to notice too that there is a direct inference in the second verse of the text that it was because of the healing ministry that people were saved. That word "because" is very significant. The people gave heed to the

Gospel message **because they saw and heard miracles.** Is not the inference very plain there that if there had been no miracles they would not have listened to the Gospel message? Do not misunderstand me brother, **the Gospel needs no miracle to back it up** and needs no healing of the body to prove its power, but it is a fact just the same that because of the glory of bodily healing, and the grace of Jesus extended toward suffering humanity, many have been born into the Kingdom of Christ that never would otherwise have called Him Lord. So if there are some of you in this great audience tonight that came to see the healing I thank God you are here! If you came to criticize I am glad my brother, that you came! If you came as a scoffer, my sister, I am glad you are in the building tonight. Perhaps in the providence of God you will experience what thousands of others have experienced, the gentle drawing magnetizing influence of the Holy Spirit calling you to this altar there to give your heart to the Lord. Jesus Christ is the same yesterday, today and forever; and if in the days of the long ago He spoke peace to troubled souls and healed their broken bodies, I believe He could do the same thing in the day in which we live.

"The Master has come over Jordan"
Said Hannah the mother one day;
"He is healing the people that throng him
With a touch of His finger, they say;
And now I shall carry my children
Little Samuel and Rachel and John,
I shall carry my sweet baby Esther
For the Savior to smile upon."

The husband looked at her kindly
But he shook his head as he smiled
Now who but a doting mother
Could think of a thing so wild?
If the children were tortured with demons
Or burning with fever, 'twere well
Or had they the taint of the leper
Like so many in Israel.

"Now do not hinder me husband,
I feel such a burden of care,
If I carry it to the dear Savior,
I know I shall leave it all there.
If He lay His hand on my children
My heart will grow lighter I know
And a blessing for ever and ever
Will follow wherever they go."

So over the hills of Judea
Along the vineyards green
With Rachel, asleep on her bosom
And Esther the brothers between
Midst the crowds that gathered around
    Him
They waited His touch of His word
Midst the row of proud Pharisees bending
She pressed to the side of her Lord.

"Now why shouldest thou trouble the
    Master,"
Said Peter, "with children like these?
Seest thou not how from morning 'till
    evening

He is touching and healing disease?
But Christ said "Forbid not the children
And suffer them to come unto Me,"
Then He took in His arms little Esther
And Rachel He sat on His knee.

Then the sad, heavy heart of the mother
Was lifted, all burdens above—
He lay His hands on the two brothers
And blessed them with tenderest love.
To the crowds that stood there around Him
As His blessing to each He had given
He said "Bring to me your dear children
For of such is the Kingdom of Heaven."

Yes, praise the Name of the Lord! He has never changed! He is just the same today and will speak to the hearts of children who are brought by the mothers of this city just as he spoke to the children in the days of long ago. What a revival! What mighty outpouring of spiritual power! What praying around the altars! What shouting of victory! What giving to God the glory! Ah, Phillip, you were true to the Master's command. You did not lost sight of the heavenly vision. You were true to your calling. Loyal to your Master's plea. You **preached Christ** unto the people and the people gave heed!

Might I state tonight that no man, in all the world can preach Christ and not get results? No man can ever tell the story of the cross and have that story, the sweetest story ever told, return unto him void. No man can challenge the integrity of God's word and the veracity of the statements of scripture—By anointing with oil and laying on hands in the name of Jesus Christ and not get some results. Unbelief was something that tied the hands of Jesus, for it is recorded that in certain cities he could do no mighty works because of their unbelief. How necessary it is for us to make a spiritual preparation and in deep and a real and a sincere consecration before we come to Him asking for the touch of His healing hand. Some time ago a train was making its way toward a great State Penitentiary. It had on board a very hardened prisoner. A man whose face had become furrowed and whose eyes had become steeled because of his life of sin. For a long time he had managed to evade the efforts of the police to catch him. Traveling from state to state and from town to town he had dodged the law, but eventually his sins found him out and he was brought to the bar of justice. Throughout his trial he maintained a very indifferent attitude and on one or two occasions was severely reprimanded by the Court for his oaths. He did not seem to care very much when the jury filed into the Court Room after considering their verdict and he was seemingly indifferent when the word "guilty" fell from the lips of the foreman. The Judge looked him in the eye as he stood to receive his sentence and when the words fell from the lips of the man on the bench, "It is the sentence of the Court that you be imprisoned for the period of 15 years," he laughed and cursed the Judge. "A hardened case," cried the policeman who had him in charge. "A tough character," said the people in the Court Room! The lawyers shook their heads and the Judge murmured, "One of the worst I have ever seen," as he climbed from the bench! On the train journey about which I am telling the train stopped at a divisional point and handcuffed to a big, burly guard, the prisoner was walking up and down the platform to get a breath of fresh air. He was manacled by the wrist and the chain that fastened him, as an animal would be fastened to the body of his keeper was plainly seen by the visitors on the station platform. A little girl about ten years of age, a sweet little innocent flower, accompanied by her mother had come to the station to say good-bye to her friend. When the eye of the child rested upon the hardened criminal she said, "Mother, what in the world are those two men chained together for?" The mother pulled her little one away for she had been carefully reared and trained in a home of refinement and have never known anything about prisons, prisoners and wardens and guards, but there is no curiosity like the curiosity of a little child and again she interrogated, "Mother you must tell me why those two men are fastened together with that big chain." "Oh," said the mother, "He is a prisoner, dearie." "And what is a prisoner?" asked the child. "You mustn't ask questions," said the mother. "Some day I will tell you all about it" she replied as she gazed into the eyes of her little darling. "But mother, I want to know now. Tell me all about it now; please, mother," and then the mother told her. She told her of the cells and the grim gray walls that keep men inside. She told her little of the sins that men have to pay for and of the wickedness for which imprisonment was a penalty. As the child gazed at the prisoner passing up and down the platform, an intense sympathy came into her little heart. She looked into the face of the man who was on his way to spend many years confined in a narrow cell and said to her mother, "Mother dear, why are they taking him away and who is going with him?" "Why, I have told you child they are taking him away because he is bad and nobody is going with him but the guard." "But who loves him," said the little one, "and who will love him after he gets to prison?" "Oh, you foolish little questioner" responded her mother. "Nobody loves a man like that. I don't presume that anybody in the world loves him. He is such a hard looking case. Come along. I don't want you to gaze at him like that." But the idea of a human being in the world with nobody to love him gripped the heart of the little girl and an inexpressible sadness stole over her countenance. Her little blue eyes dimmed with tears. No one to love him! No one to care for him! Just a hard case! A poor prisoner on his way to jail! Something rose within her throat and some impulse stirred her as she grabbed a rose from the bouquet her mother carried and before her astonished mother could stop her she sped swiftly across the platform and handed the rose to the amazed prisoner and stammered, "I, I l-love you, and God loves you too." She turned on her heel and ran back as swiftly as she went. The scene changes.

Sunday in the penitentiary. The chapel service was over and the message of the day has been delivered. The prisoners had gone back to their cells or were lounging around in the yard where they were allowed some liberty Sunday afternoon. The Christian Endeavor Society service was about to commence and as the prisoners filed into the room the evangelist noticed that no guard attended them and they all seemed to be placed upon their honor. The prison band made its appearance and soon the room in which the service was held resounded to the strains of "Jesus Lover of My Soul" sung to the tune of "Silver Threads Among the Gold." A fine looking man in prison uniform was behind the sacred desk. After the strains of the hymn, sung entirely by the voices of men, had died away, the prisoner arose and led in prayer. His deep tones rang through the building. A silence prevailed and the assembled prisoners with closed eyes followed him as he read. Sincerity was heard in every word. A love for Christ was felt as he talked to the men of

Galilee; poor fellow. Behind the bars. A prisoner undoubtedly paying the penalty for his misdeeds. The visitor mused, and the chaplain noticing the evangelist's interest said, "I will tell you his story."

It was not until the service was over and the men had bene dismissed that he got the story from the chaplain. "Some time ago," said he, "I was walking along the corridors of the prison and glanced through the bars to see one of the new arrivals sitting on his bed with a Bible open on his knee. His reputation had preceded him to the penitentiary and they called him a hard case, and said he had a heart of stone! There he sat with an open Bible before him, the only book he was allowed to keep in his cell night and day. I noticed his pensive attitude, and as I passed he looked appealingly into my eyes. Thinking he was interested in some part of the Bible, I asked the turnkey to let me into his cell. Sitting down by his side on the bed I slipped my arm around his shoulder and talked to him of the Lord. To my amazement he brushed back my hand and looked into my face, opened the book that he had closed and there between its pages I saw the petals of a red rose that he had crushed. Tears filled his eyes as he said with a broken voice, "The little kid. Chaplain, the little kid! She come up to me at the station, and she gives me this flower and she says, 'I love you, and God loves you too!' Nobody ever talked to me like that. I just can't figure it out Chaplain! Can't figure it out no ways at all." The Chaplain with an avenue of approach now open, **preached Christ unto him.** No room there for a lecture on evolution. No time there for a treatise on philosophy. **He preached Christ.** The prison walls were thick. The prison bars were strong, but they could not keep out the Man of Galilee that day.

Concluding his narrative the Chaplain said he had been his right hand support. More than one fellow during the years of his imprisonment has he led to the Christ and more than one man knows the glory and the power of real salvation because of his personal work. So you see, my brother, that Phillip preached the message that alone can bring results. He preached Christ unto the people. Let me conclude by saying that the scripture states there **was great joy in that city.** There will be great joy in **this city** when the people receive Jesus! There will be happiness in the homes of hundreds, joy in the lives of thousands, when the Man of Galilee takes up His abode in their hearts! There is not a heart that is broken but what He can heal; not a life that is sad but what He can fill it with joy; not a sorrow but what He can lift it; not a burden but what He will bear it; so tonight, whatever your need, I ask you to come to Jesus and before the campaign is over and the lights are turned out in this great Arena and this campaign shall have passed into history, there will be joy in your hearts, joy in the city, and joy in the presence of angels of God over every sinner that repenteth. Hallelujah! Glory and honor, majesty and power is ascribed unto the Christ we preach.

BONUS CONTENT!

Following are two chapters from another of Price's classic works, titled:

The Meaning of Faith

While we could have place any number of writings by Price in this volume, it seemed right to include a couple of extra chapters on the subject of divine healing.

If you'd like to read the rest of the book, it's available through our website.

JawboneDigital.com/Price

CHAPTER 10
FAITH IN DIVINE HEALING

We now come to a subject of vital interest: namely, the question of divine healing.

Nobody knows more than I do the tremendous protest that the ministry of divine healing has brought about in the Church of the day in which we live. When some years ago a great revival wave of the ministry of divine healing encircled the entire globe, it was not long until the opposition began to be organized, and every honest and dishonest means was used to try to persuade people against it. Books were written by the score; sarcastic articles filled the columns of the newspapers; and even religious magazines devoted page after page to tirades against the ministry of divine healing. I believe the devil was mad. I believe that he was so angry that he commenced to use every weapon at his command to stamp out the belief in the supernatural power of God relative to the healing of the body.

The revival of divine healing ministry came at the close of the Philadelphian age of the church. It was nothing but a natural result of the glory and power of the Philadelphian era of evangelism and holiness. Practically every one of the great denominational leaders who were stalwarts of the faith were hearty believers in divine healing, and many of them claimed to have been delivered from physical infirmities by the power of God. John Wesley filled his journal with it. Andrew Murray wrote a book about it. John Knox practiced it and preached it as he went like a firebrand through Scotland. Peter Cartwright proclaimed it. In later years men of the intellectual caliber and spiritual power of A.T. Pierson championed this gospel truth.

There was not the slightest doubt about it —people were healed by the power of God. It was proving to be one of the greatest forces for the salvation of souls and for the spreading of the fires of evangelism that the

Church had seen for centuries.

No wonder the devil was mad. People could behold with their eyes the mighty works of God. Altars were filled with men and women seeking Jesus Christ as a personal Savior. They were not all after loaves and fishes by any means. When a man testified that he had been changed in soul and in heart, they had nothing to go on except his word of testimony until perhaps his life began to prove his testimony; but when the lame man commenced to leap and the lips of the dumb were loosed—even sinful men opened their eyes in wonderment, and the world began to know that there was a God in Israel. As it was in the days of the apostles that people came running together because they heard of the healings that had taken place, so it began to happen in the days in which we live.

The ultimate aim of a public divine healing ministry was not only to get men healed in body, but to get them to God for the salvation of their souls. The salvation of the soul is of infinitely more importance than the healing of the body. What shall it profit a man if he gain a well body and lose his own soul? Beginning on the day after Pentecost, the disciples, filled with the Holy Ghost and full of faith and of the power of God, began to pray for the sick. They used divine healing as a means of drawing the people and then preaching to them the gospel of a God of marvelous love. No wonder that the fires of revival swept across continents, leaped over the seas, and invaded the isles everywhere.

There is no doubt in my mind but that this was God's plan. He used it then, and if it was legitimate then it certainly would meet with the divine approval now. But years ago John beheld in the spirit the tragedy that was to take place during the closing days of time. While he was sitting on the lonely Isle of Patmos listening to the surging of the sad sea waves, God gave him that glorious and wonderful revelation that supersedes any spiritual revelation of its kind ever given to man. John beheld a radiant church, glorious and wonderful to behold, standing on the mountain peaks of a Philadelphian experience, begin to succumb to the bombardments of the enemy.

It was not the devil of lust that led his force against the citadels. It was not the devil of drink or of vice that stormed the Philadelphian heights. The soldiery of hell wore no armor but instead they clothed themselves with the equipment of the preacher and dipped their tongues in honey as they spoke. The devil sent his emissaries of reason and wisdom and they declared, "Hail, Philadelphia, we have come to thee in the name of the Lord. We are the revealers of truth that you have never discovered. We are the heralds of knowledge such as you have never known. We are friends of God and we wish to unfold to you the deeper understanding—the rational interpretation of the Word that you have never comprehended before."

Philadelphia began to capitulate. It soon closed its prayer meeting to listen to the lectures on science. Then somebody asked for faith, but faith had gone. The light was slowly flickering out and it was easy for it to be enticed along the road of new research until at last it found itself in the vales of Laodicea. It kept up the old forms. It sang hymns—it prayed prayers such as they were—it built the same kind of buildings; but something was gone. Or rather it was Somebody. It was the power and the presence of the Holy Ghost. So evangelism left the pulpit and reason climbed the rostrum steps. So faith was banished from the councils and intellectualism started to preach. There was no salvation through the blood, no bodily ascension of the Lord, no personal appearing of Jesus in the clouds of glory—these things were all gone. As for divine healing, if ever there was any, it was for a bygone age.

If anybody testified to the fact that they were healed, the Pharisees of the closing days said, "He casteth out devils by Beelzebub, the prince of the devils."

Mothers have come to me with tears streaming down their cheeks, weeping because of the growing unbelief of their sons and daughters. Young men and young women in their teens have sat by my desk and laughed in my face as I have told them that I still believe in the verbal inspiration of the good old Book and all the accounts that are contained therein of the supernatural power of God. They laugh at Mother and call her old-fashioned, and they ridicule Father and declare that he is an old fogy in his religious beliefs, even though he might be a pretty good dad. The modernistic preacher backs them up and declares that we must have a gospel that will fit in with the college needs of this particular day.

What a tragedy! The angels of Heaven must hide their faces as they contemplate such an awful sight. As for myself, I would rather have never known the way—never to have mounted a pulpit step—than to be in the shoes of one of those intellectual giants who have contributed to the spiritual delinquency of the youth of our day. They preach loudly and long about the wrecking of the body while they destroy faith in God and proceed to wreck the soul.

My dear young friend, if such you are into whose hands this book shall fall, let me give you one word of irrefutable logic. The proof of the pudding is in the eating. The proof of the gospel is in what it does. The proof of the Bible is in the fact of the fulfillment of its promises. There might be some basis for your doubt if you prayed to a God who never answered. If there was never a reply, no matter how intently you prayed, then you might have some basis for your assumption that there is no God. When you pray and He answers, you know there must be a God. When you pray for healing and healing comes, then you know there must be a Healer somewhere.

With all of my heart I assure you that if you will be honest enough and sincere enough to come, even in your doubt and in your fear, God Himself will recognize the little flickering flame of integrity and sincerity that I know must lie within your breast.

Let me give you this challenge. By following out what the Bible tells you to do, you will experience just what the Bible says you will experience. God is His own interpreter and He will make plain those spiritual truths that you never have hitherto grasped.

So it is in the realm of divine healing. While others defame and scatter the seeds of doubt and fear—God is still healing people. There are tens of thousands of them who are living today who can testify to the miraculous and supernatural healing power of Jehovah-Rapha. Many of these cases are so evident that even the bitterest enemies of Divine Healing have had to admit that the people have been healed. Oh, how real and wonderful Jesus is to the man who has felt His healing touch! But they deny that a loving healing Savior did it.

CHAPTER 11
FAITH FOR HEALING

The humanity of Jesus overwhelms me—His understanding of our human nature, His great tender heart, His infinite and beautiful compassion. He never would break the bruised reed and no account in Scripture tells us that He ever quenched the smoking flax. The broken heart He never despised, and the faintest cry always found lodgment in His sympathetic ear.

Did ever a man speak as this man spoke? Did ever a heart love as this heart loved? He, who was God, wrapped around His deity the garments of humanity and placed a human hand upon many a fevered brow. Wonderful Jesus—very image of the Father—who came to make the healing waters flow where every thirsty heart could drink. Wonderful, wonderful Jesus!

The records are simply filled with the story

of His healing ministry. The Bible is very clear about them—they were miracles of healing for the physical body. In the second place, He distinctly told His disciples that they were to continue in the ministry of healing that He was imparting to them. In clear and plain language they were told that they were to lay hands on the sick and that they should recover. As a matter of fact, it was to be one of the signs that were to follow them that believe. The Scripture is so clear and so plain that a child can understand it. It receives all the authority it needs for the words were spoken by Jesus Christ Himself.

In the next place, after the death, resurrection, and ascension of Jesus, the disciples did exactly what the Lord told them to do. They prayed for the sick and the sick were healed. The Book of Acts is filled with accounts of the miracle-working power of God in relation to the restoration of health to the bodies of men who were sick. In the various epistles divine healing is very clearly taught, and the first president of the first ministerial union that ever convened, the apostle James, wrote plainly and forcefully regarding the position of the Church in this respect. James 5:14 still stands as a lighthouse upon a hill, shining out its welcome beams of truth to every child of God who is suffering from bodily ailment and pain. The lightnings have flashed, the thunders have rolled, the storms of unbelief have reached around the foot of the rock; but the light still shines. There was James 5:14 at the end of the apostolic era and there is still James 5:14 in the day in which we live. Devils in hell, unbelieving men, and faithless preachers have all failed to put out that light.

The Pauline Epistles bring further and added corroboration to those great truths. The ministry of the apostle himself was simply filled with manifestations of the power of Christ to heal.

I understand from the Word itself that no man could ever add to or take away from the words of the completed Book. It is the direct teaching of the Lord that even the Spirit

Himself would never again fall on man in such a way as to cause him to add to the inspired Word. God's revealed will as far as the Bible is concerned has been completed and is final. No man has ever been authorized by the Spirit or by virtue of his own understandings to take away from the completed and inspired Word of God.

I would like to ask the critics of divine healing for the chapter and verse in which it is declared that divine healing would ever be taken away from the Church, or that the hour would ever arrive when it would be against God's will for us to pray for the sick. I challenge them to give me one scintilla of scriptural evidence that would lead any man to believe that the commands of the Lord would ever be abrogated and the teachings of the apostle nullified in this respect. They cannot do it, and they know they cannot do it. So they rise up and say—half of a verse is for yesterday and half of a verse is for today. They tell you to take this and throw out that. Who gave them the authority to wield the scissors of criticism on the inspired page? From what source did they get their authority to take from the Word of God?

Here is where faith comes in. Faith—glorious faith—God-imparted faith—looks up of times through scalding tears and, holding the Word of the Lord high in its hand toward Heaven, says, "Lord, I believe." When the part can contain the whole, then the mind of man can understand the Bible without the help of the Holy Spirit. When time is longer than eternity, then reason should dethrone faith and establish itself as the emperor of our lives. These things can never be.

There is only one possible way of clearing out the debris and the rubbish of unbelief and of modernistic interpretation from the rooms of our hearts, and that is by the exercise of faith in God. Without the slightest hesitation I declare that the man who wants faith can have it. If we are sinners we need not cry in vain. God Himself will fulfill the promises because He perfected the plan. The man who wants to know, by the grace of God can know. Light can shine in the darkest place and understanding can come to the heart that has been clouded by the fogs of unbelief.

We are not swayed by any self-desire—we are not moved by any sentiment when we arrive at the conclusion that divine healing is a blessing that has been provided by the Lord Jesus Himself. Once again we repeat that faith must be founded upon evidence and must be grounded on something that is strong enough to nourish it and to sustain it.

When we consider the ground work of our faith when it comes to the healing of the body, every poor sufferer should shout for joy. It is the shout that brings the victory. It is the anthem of joy that will make the walls fall down. It would be wonderful indeed were we to pray for physical deliverance, basing our prayer upon some promise of the Word of God. There is a sense in which we do that. But it is far more wonderful to believe that we can appropriate our physical healing because it has already been purchased for us through the atoning ministry of Jesus.

Divine healing is undoubtedly an integral part of the atoning work of the Lord Jesus Christ. Next time you meet around that sacred table with your brethren who form the body of your church—which is the Body of Christ—I want you to ask yourselves solemnly and sincerely a few very important questions. Why did Jesus differentiate between the wine and the bread? Why did He say, "This is My blood" and then again, "This is My body"? If the blood was shed for the remission of sins was there any need for the body to be broken for the same cause? It was a statement of Jesus that the blood was shed for them, and in addition to that, the body was broken for them.

The word that is in the very heart and core of the meaning of the atonement is the word substitutional. From Genesis to Revelation the Bible rings in type and anti-type with the declaration of this glorious truth. Why is it that I shall live eternally? Because Jesus died my death. Why is it that I can walk in holiness before Him? Because He took all of my sins.

Why is it that I am redeemed and saved from the guilt of iniquity? Because Jesus not only bore my guilt and carried my sins in the judgment hall of Pontius Pilate, but He carried them before the tribunals of God.

Why is it that we are instructed in the Word by the apostle Paul to rejoice in the Lord? Because Jesus carried all of our grief. Why is it that we are instructed not to be anxious about the things of the present? Because He lifted our anxiety and gave us His promises for the future.

As He took my sin, He gave me His sinlessness. When He assumed my guilt He gave me His holiness. Beloved, the whole super-structure of the doctrine of the atonement would crumble if you took out of the foundation those two glorious words substitutional and vicarious. It must of necessity follow then that if substitution is a cardinal doctrine of the atonement as regards deliverance from sin, it must also be an essential doctrine with regard to deliverance from disease. In other words—if it is true that

Jesus carried our sins in atoning for them, then He must of necessity have carried our sicknesses too, if He was going to atone for them in the same way.

One thing is very sure—if healing is not in the atonement then the Christian can only pray for it as a privilege; but if it is in the atonement he can claim it as a heritage. If it is not in the atonement the question of healing becomes a matter of intercession. If it is in the atonement it becomes a matter of appropriation. How can anybody appropriate without faith? By no stretch of the imagination would it be possible for anybody to become the recipient of the blessing except by faith.

You tell me that God could just give it to you without any exercise of faith on your part? That is what a great many people expect God to do. But He does not work that way. If He did that, would you ever seek His face? Would you ever pray? Would you ever draw away from the humdrum of this world and alone in your closet lift your hands to God?

Some of you would not even take the trouble to read your Bible—and if God would visit you with health and heal your sickness, you would not even stop to thank Him for it. I know human nature well enough to be able to make that statement.

A man once contradicted a similar statement I made. He declared that under no circumstances would there be a human being on the face of the earth that would be ungrateful enough as not to thank the Lord if he became the recipient of such a blessing as that. I had dinner with that same man and he never took the time to thank the Lord for the food. As I passed him the bread and potatoes I told him that I was giving him two miracles of God's genius and power. He told me that he grew the potatoes and bought the bread—but what could he have done without God? During the conversation I unfolded the message that God brought to my heart while walking around in his grassy fields.

In that pasture were horses, cows, chickens, pigs, and sheep. They were all eating the same grass. They were all drinking the same water. The same identical water and food was somehow changed to strength in the horse, milk in the cow, eggs in the chicken, wool on the back of the sheep and bacon in the pigs. I then asked my friend if he did not think that was a miracle. He answered that it was nature. But back of what we call the natural is the supernatural. Back of the created is the Creator. To have one you must have the other. He then admitted that it was a miracle. God was behind the food on the table, the clothes on his back, the wood with which his house was built. He was even the Giver of the water that was in the glass by his side. Then I asked him why he did not thank God for them. He made no reply. But there will come a day when he will answer that question.

Thus concludes your book.

Be sure to visit us online for more of the best Christian books ever written, including many more by **Charles S. Price**.

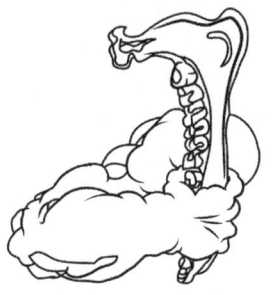

http://JawboneDigital.com/Price

Made in the USA
Coppell, TX
13 November 2019